The 12 Steps of Photography

Shawn M. Tomlinson's Guide to Photography
Volume 3

by

shawn m tomlinson

2015

The 12 Steps of Photography

A Guide for Getting Good At Your Passion

Shawn M. Tomlinson's
Guide to Photography
Volume 3

ISBN: 978-1-329-31572-3

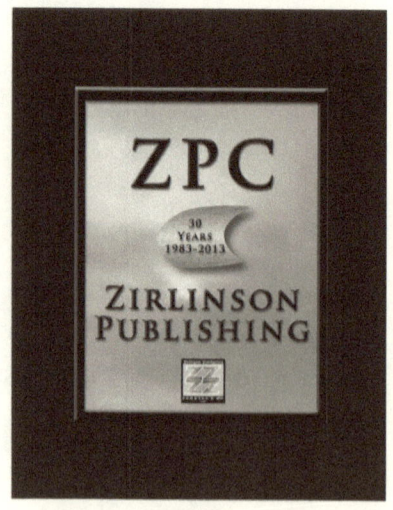

The 12 Steps of Photography

Shawn M. Tomlinson's
Guide to Photography
Volume 3

by

shawn m tomlinson

2015

Introduction

Everybody gives out tips for better photography.

Well, maybe not your boss or the guy who fixes your furnace (although mine does), but most photography websites, forums and magazines — the few that are left — fill their pages with tips for becoming a better photographer.

There's a reason there are so many tips out there — although most of them cover the same things — and that's that photographers — especially novice photographers — want them.

On the other hand, we who have some little knowledge like to give them, too. Most people like to pass on what they've learned.

I've been a photographer for nearly four decades. I've published thousands of photographs. I write a photography column (Photo Curmudgeon). I love photography.

In case that wasn't clear.

I read tips from other photographers often. Sometimes, I read something new, or at least put in a new way so that it sparks an idea.

A lot of tip articles tend to say the same things, if you read many of them. And, let's face it, there are just so many things to say and to learn.

No one — including me — can tell you how to develop your photographer's eye. Only you can figure that out. What works for me won't necessarily work for you, and vice versa. The way I see through a camera viewfinder is different than the way you see.

What I can do, though, is give you some pointers about how to develop your own photographer's eye, and how to get better as a photographer.

Come on along.

A Note on the Photographs

I shoot with five of my own DSLRs as of this writing. I also occasionally shoot with a borrowed camera, and I've had a couple that had to be returned because of flaws and were replaced with something else. I include in this book photos from virtually every DSLR I've shot with for a couple of reasons. First, they illustrate the points in the book, and second they are presented to prove that megapixels don't matter as much as many people think. Here you will find images from the Nikon D1 at 2.65 megapixels, the Nikon D1X at 5.47 mp, the Pentax *ist DS, Canon 10D and Nikon D70 at 6.1 mp, the Canon EOS 20D at 8.2 mp, the Pentax K20D at 14.2 mp, the Nikon D7000 at 16.2 mp and the Nikon D3200 at 24 megapixels. The resolution of the camera along with exposure details are included for each photograph.

Smash Your Smartphone

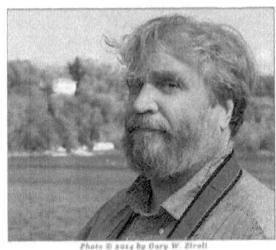

Photo © 2014 by Gary W. Ziroli

The 12 Steps of Photography

Step 1

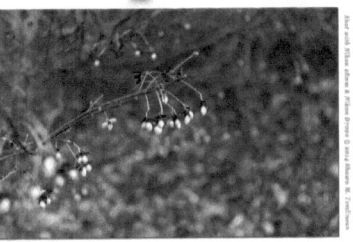

If you use your smartphone as a camera, take it out right now and smash it to tiny bits. Or at least smash out the lens.

Smartphones have replaced the point-and-shoot cameras to such an extent that the point-and-shoot market is in serious trouble.

And we don't care about that.

Whether you are shooting your images with a point-and-shoot or a smartphone, you are depriving yourself of, well, being a photographer.

Anyone can point a smartphone at something and capture an image. Everyone does.

Fine, OK.

But you want to be a *photographer*, right? Or you consider yourself one already?

Smash your smartphone.

Yes, they're expensive, so, OK, if you don't want to smash yours, get a family member to perform an intervention and remove your smartphone from you and keep it from you or at least monitor your use so you don't feel the urge to shoot a photo with it.

Consider yourself addicted and take the necessary steps to go into recovery.

If you do it this way, you will have your smartphone — and most people can't seem to live without them now — once you have learned moderation. Sure, someday, you may again want to take a photo with

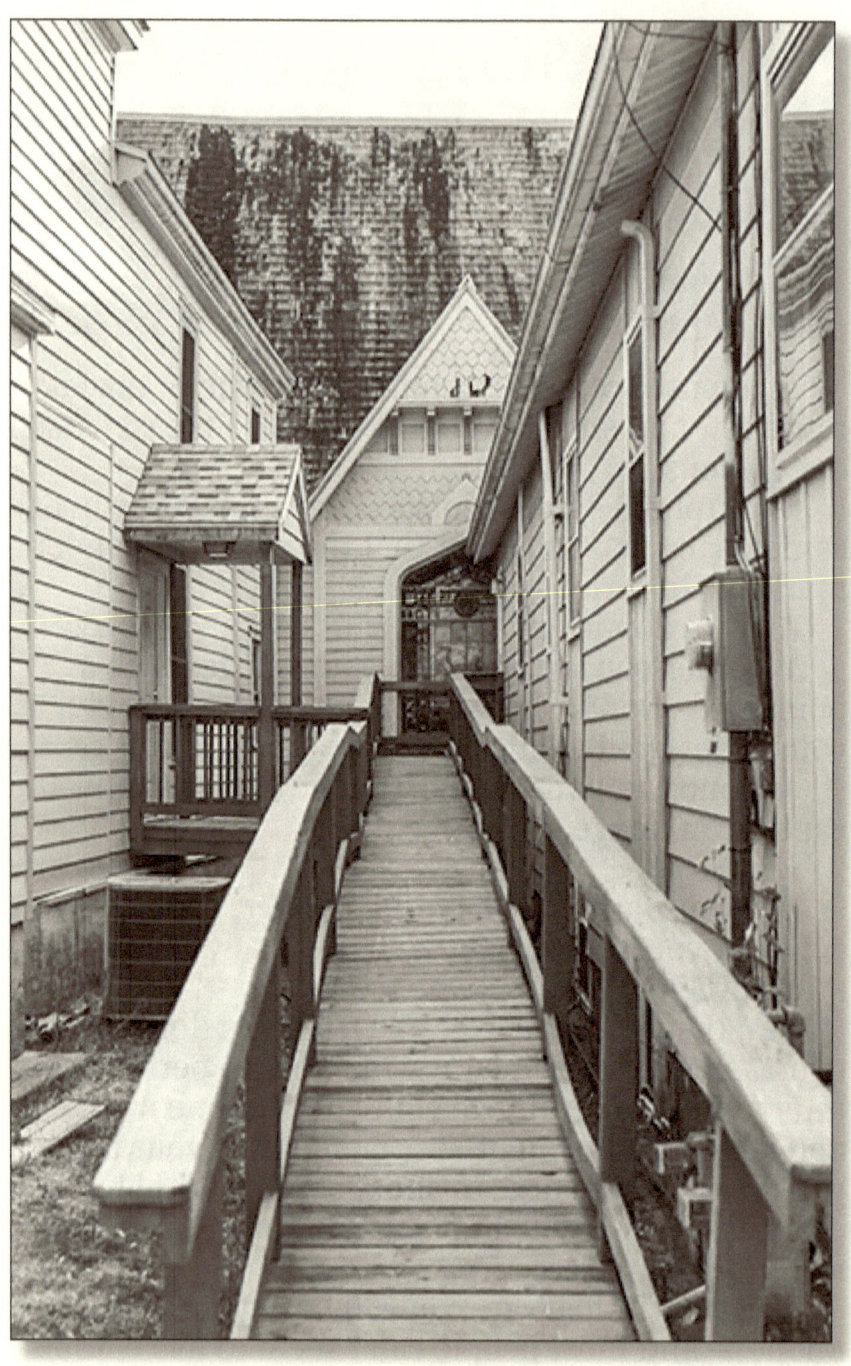

Saratoga Springs, N.Y., Nov. 25, 2014.
Nikon D7000 (16.2 megapixels), 28 mm (prime), 1/800, f/2.8, ISO 400
© 2014, 2015 by Shawn M. Tomlinson

your smartphone, but — trust me — it will diminish once you have become a "photographer."

The reason for all this pseudo-drama is that smartphones produce OK photos, but if that's all you're looking for, then you can stop reading now. Go off and have a merry life.

If you want something more from photography than slapping an Instagram filter on your snapshot and spamming everyone you know with it, then it's time to stop thinking of your smartphone as a camera.

Sure, shoot some video with it if you like. Smartphones are fairly good at that, unless you want to be a cinematographer, in which case, see the above about smashing your smartphone.

I'm not saying you'll never get a great photo from a smartphone. You may. And that may cause you a problem. Consider this. You take the greatest single image ever taken with your iPhone. No one has ever seen anything like it. It's amazing. It brings tears and joy at the same time to all those who see it. It becomes so famous that the Metropolitan calls you to beg you to let them display it in the grand entranceway to the museum.

That's where your problem begins.

Despite advances in smartphone photo quality, the truth is, the images only look really good on a very small screen, that of, say, a smartphone. Once you try to enlarge and print the image, you will find there are some problems. Like red-green-blue noise artifacts and grain or "bumpiness" and really fuzzy images.

To get a real photograph from your work, you need real equipment. It really doesn't matter which brand you choose; Nikon, Pentax, Canon, Sony, etc. all produce great images. What matters is the type of camera you choose from any of these companies.

Oh sure, if you're loaded — rich, not drunk; or well, both — you can spend $30,000 on a Hasselblad or $7,000 on a Leica, but most of us can't or at least don't want to do that. Well, OK, we want to but... not yet. If you do have the money, these types of cameras are fantastic, but you still have to be good at being a photographer to see that in the images.

And, mirrorless... hmmm... well, you can go that way, and some are, but mirrorless cameras still are not the primary choice. They may be one day, but not yet.

For serious photography — for enthusiasts and pros — the only real choice is the digital single-lens reflex camera, otherwise known as a DSLR.

These types of cameras emerged in the 1950s with film cameras, and when everyone started the move to digital, the basic design remained. That's just how good the design is.

A DSLR works like this: The camera body contains a mirror and a sensor in the center, behind the lens mount. The image enters the lens, hits the mirror and bounces upward to what's called a pentaprism. The pentaprism fixes the way you see the image. Straight from the lens, the image would be upside down and reversed left-to-right. The pentaprism corrects this so that what you see in the viewfinder is what you would see without the camera. You compose the image, set the settings and press the shutter release button. The mirror flips up, the sensor activates and captures the image, then the mirror flips back down into place for the next image.

The primary advantage of the DSLR is that, because you compose your image through the same lens that captures the image, you can use a wide variety of

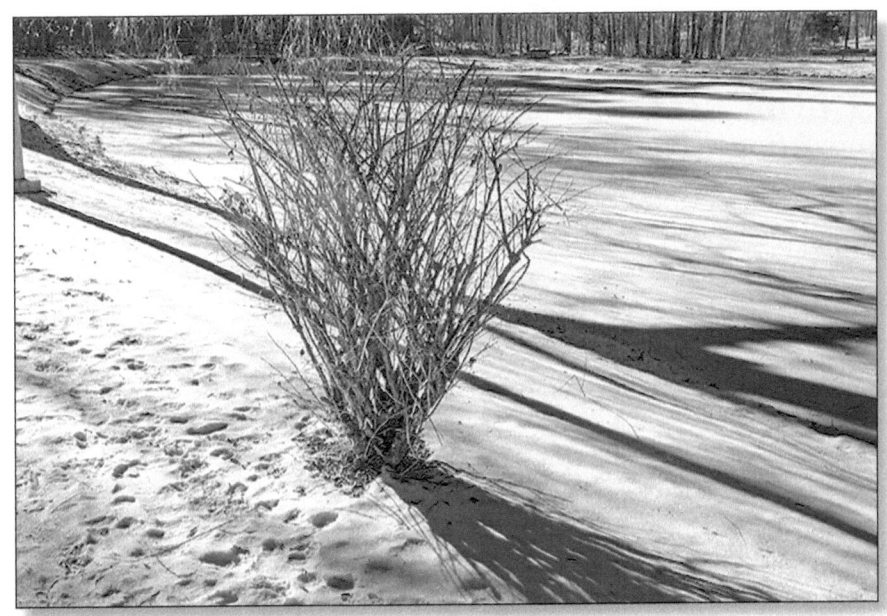

Wolfarth's Pond Park, Gloversville, N.Y., Nov. 21, 2014.
Nikon D7000, 28 mm (prime), 1/500, f/11, ISO 400
© 2014, 2015 by Shawn M. Tomlinson

lenses. Unlike other camera types — point-and-shoots and rangefinders — there is no parallax, a difference in angle between the viewfinder and the lens.

The second advantage is that camera manufacturers and their designers and engineers put the majority of their effort into making DSLR cameras because the pros want them. And serious amateurs and enthusiasts want them, and that's where the money is.

That means that even entry-level DSLRs are the forefront of digital photography technology.

You may think this means you need to rush right out and get the latest, snazziest DSLR, but you don't really. You can, and certainly you will have the latest technology. But if the cost puts you off and keeps you thinking, "I'll never have the money to buy the camera I really want, so I can't be a photographer, so I'm going to sit in the corner and cry," don't worry about it.

In my *Retro Camera Buying Guide: Getting Serious About Photography... On the Cheap!* book, I give the basics of how to buy good older DSLRs that will do almost everything newer ones will for a lot less money. Less than $250 for a camera body, lens, gadget bag and accessories.

Anyway, smash your smartphone and let's get to it.

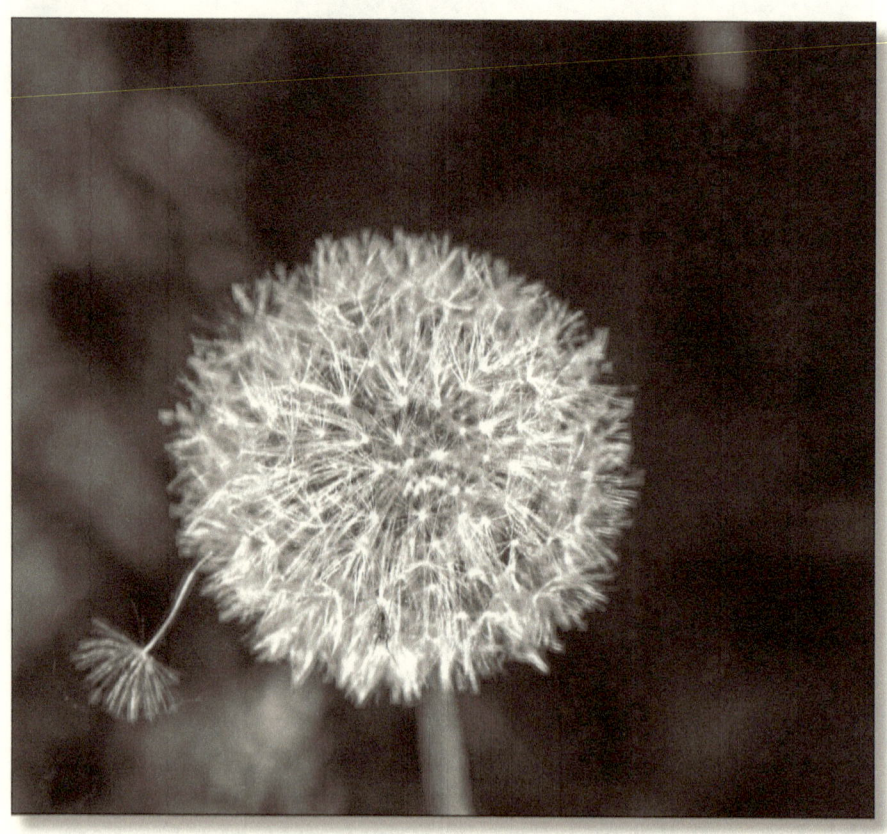

Ballston Lake, N.Y., May 18, 2015.
Nikon D2x, 300mm, 1/800, f/5.6, ISO 400, Tv, Pattern Metering
Photo © 2015 by Shawn M. Tomlinson

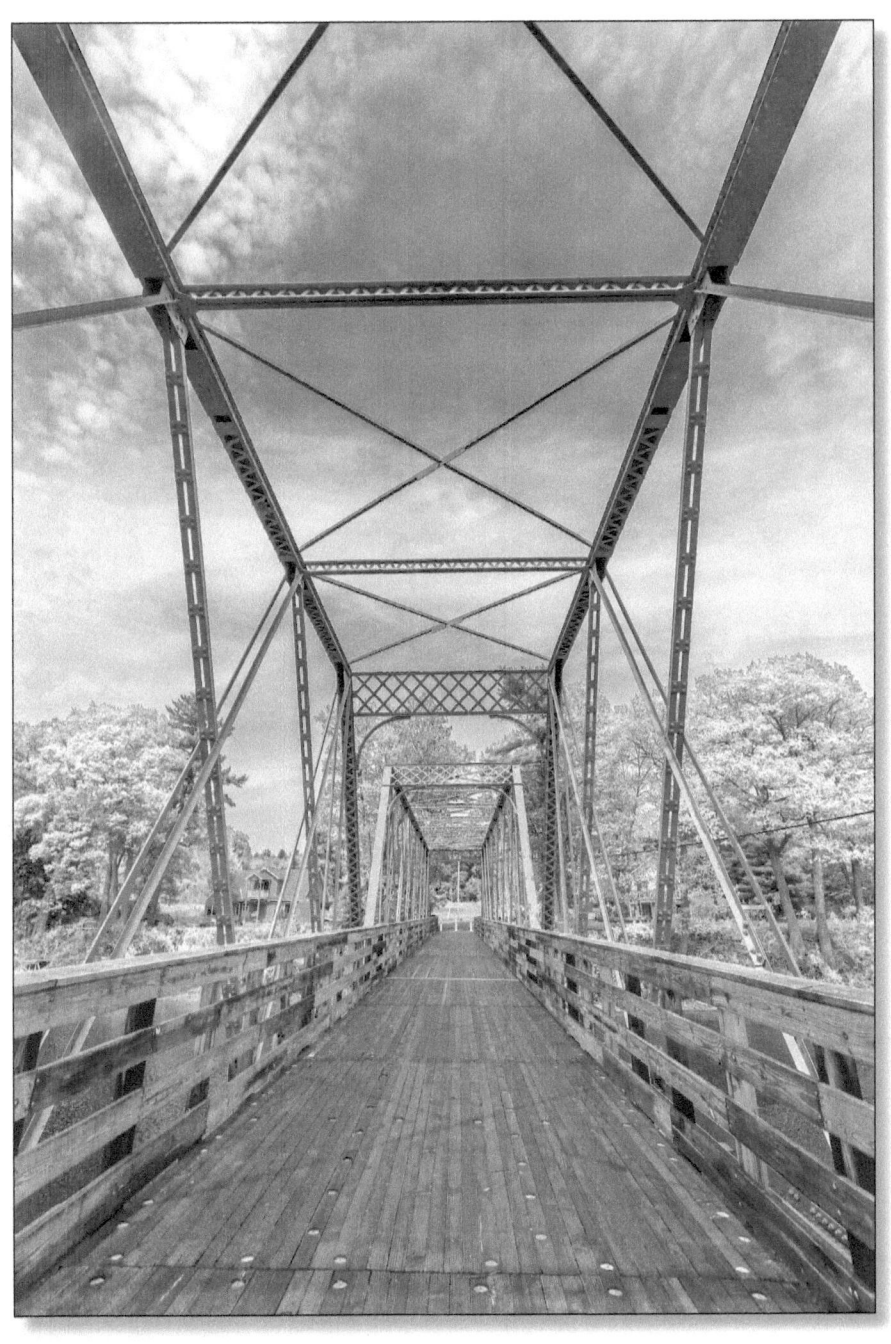

Schuylerville, N.Y., May 16, 2015.
Nikon D7000, 10mm, 1/800, f/9, ISO 320, Tv, Pattern Metering
Photo © 2015 by Shawn M. Tomlinson

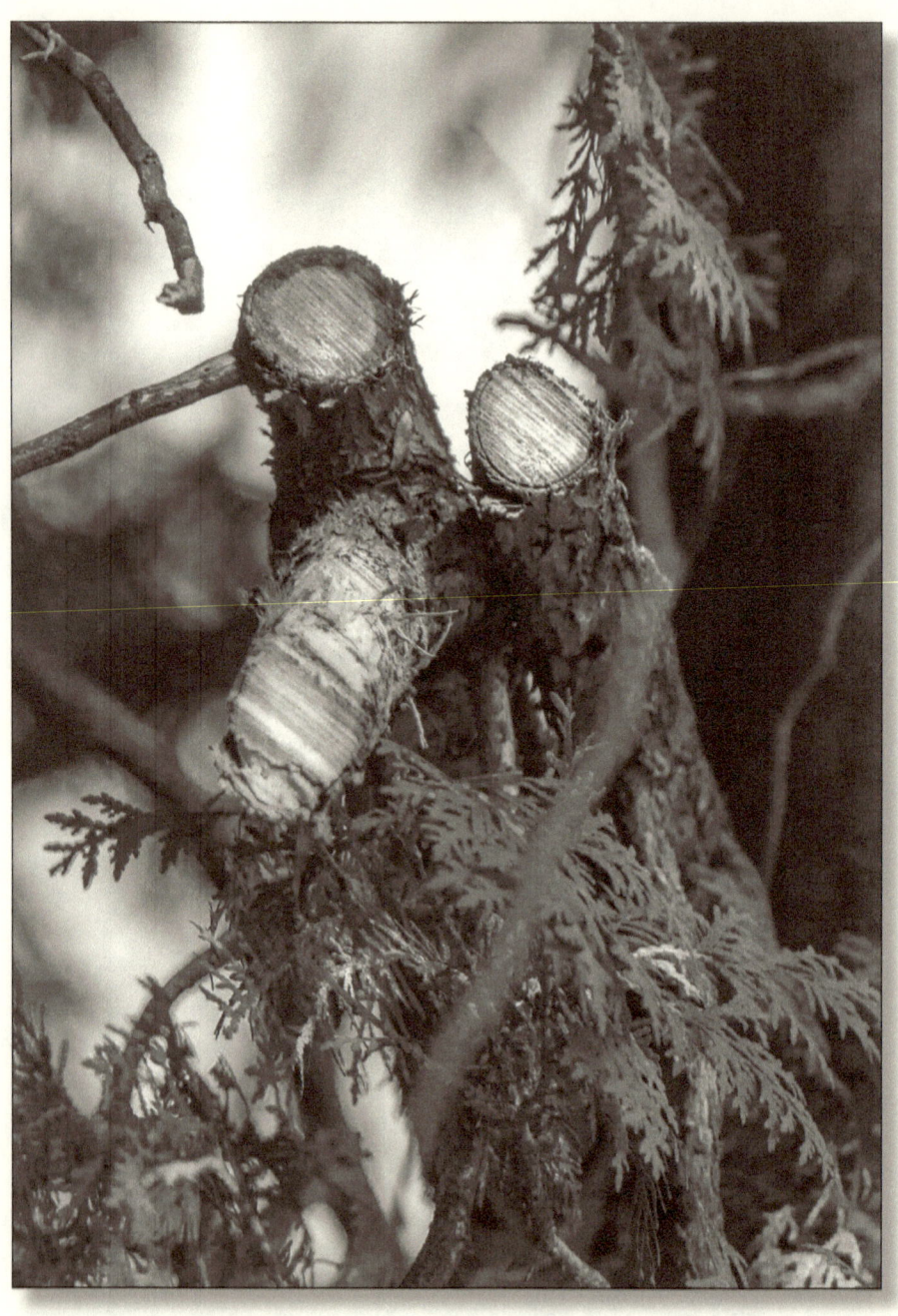

Italian Gardens, Broadalbin, N.Y., Aug. 16, 2014.
Nikon D70 (6.1 megapixels), 300mm, 1/1000, f/6, ISO 400
© 2014, 2015 by Shawn M. Tomlinson

Go RAW

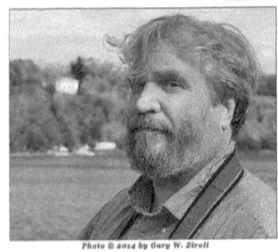

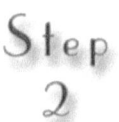

The 12 Steps of Photography

Step 2

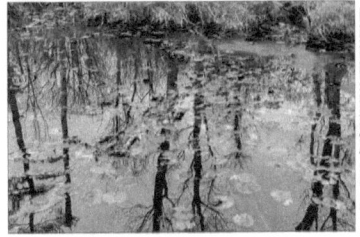

Photo © 2014 by Gary W. Ziroli

Another major advantage of DSLRs over point-and-shoots and your now-in-pieces smartphone is that you can shoot in RAW.

RAW is a file format that records virtually every bit of information in an instant for each photo. This is very important. I can't stress it enough.

Why?

When you shoot in JPEG several things happen. The DSLR's "brain" works to come up with a "pretty good" rendition of what you shot, meaning it balances things according to the exposure you or the camera sets. This results in a flat looking image with very limited dynamic range, meaning the colors, sharpness, saturation and contrast are a balance and therefore "pretty good" but not necessarily what you would like to get from your photography. The DSLR's brain also compresses the image. That's what JPEG is, a file format for compressing images. The only way it can do this is by throwing bits of digital information away. This, too, does several things. It adds to that flat look. It removes information that must have been recorded for some reason. It adds artifacts — particularly red-green-blue noise — especially in the shadows and other darker areas.

Because JPEG files are compressed, you can get more of them on a memory card than RAW files. Don't let that tempt you. You will regret it later.

Case in point. My first DSLR was a Pentax *ist DS. I still use it because it's a great camera, even a decade on. It's a great camera, but I wasn't a great or at least knowledgeable photographer in 2005 when I bought it.

Two things entered into this equation.

First, I started in photography with film cameras and used them for many years. Since I shot a lot of stuff for newspapers, I needed flexible film that would work outdoors in daylight and indoors under poor lighting conditions. That led me to

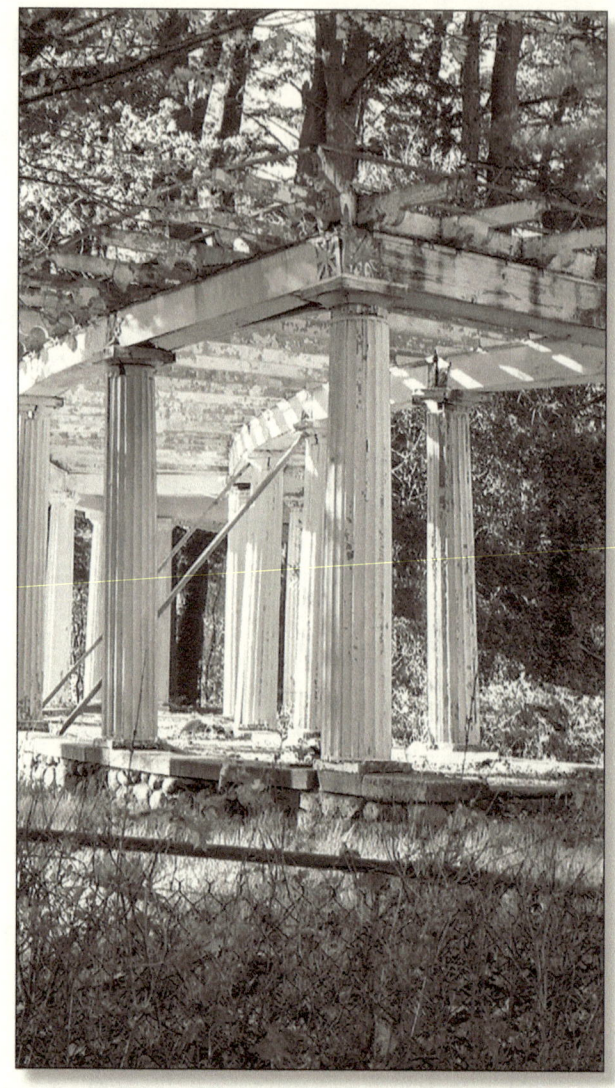

Italian Gardens, Broadalbin, N.Y., May 12, 2005.
Pentax *ist DS (6.1 megapixels), 35 mm, 1/250, f/10, ISO 1600
© 2005, 2015 by Shawn M. Tomlinson

the compromise of 400 ASA film, color and black and white. I shot with it 95 percent of the time. So, in my head, the higher the ASA — which became ISO when it was still film and translated to the light sensitivity measurement in digital cameras — the better.

Second, in 2005, SecureDigital (SD) cards were expensive. I paid nearly $90 for a 1gb SanDisk.

So, I got my new and spiffy DSLR, paid my $90 for that 1gb SD card, put it in and set it to RAW just like my photographer buddies all told me to. On the 6-megapixel Pentax *ist DS, a 1gb SD card could record 92 images.

That didn't seem like much. It gave fewer images than three rolls of 36-exposure film.

However, when I changed it to JPEG —

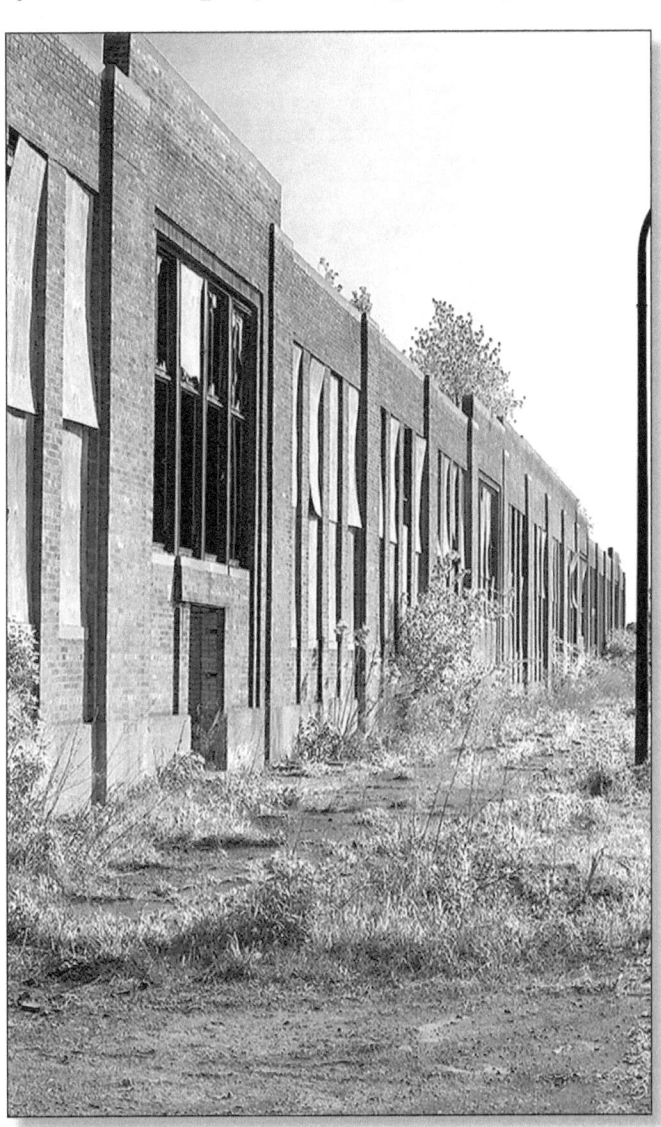

Buffalo Central Terminal, Buffalo, N.Y., May 28, 2005.
Pentax *ist DS (6.1 megapixels), 35 mm, 1/1000, f/11, ISO 1600
© 2005, 2015 by Shawn M. Tomlinson

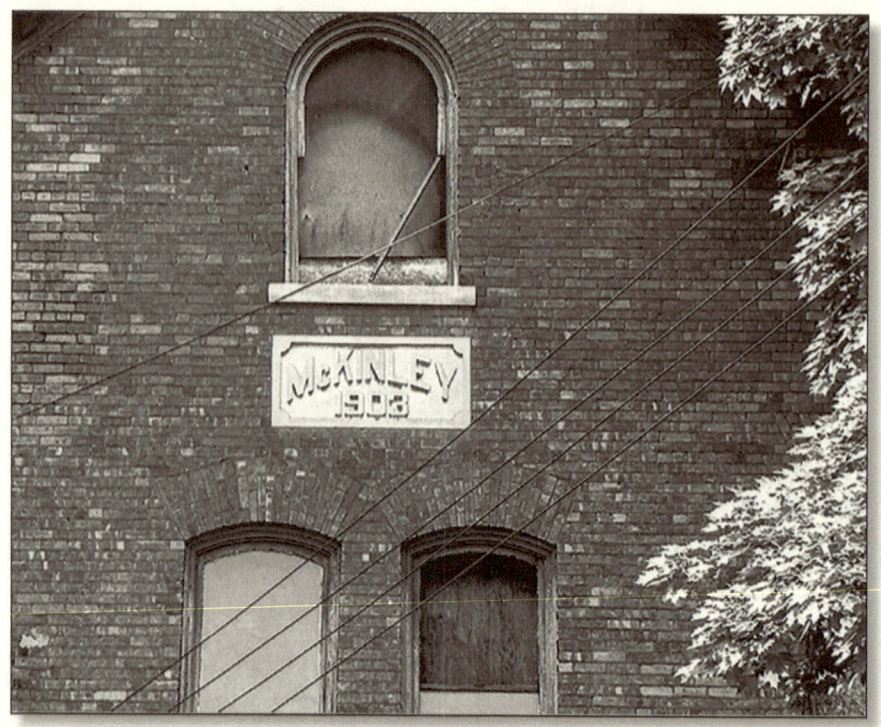

Gloversville, N.Y., June 2, 2005.
Pentax *ist DS (6.1 megapixels), 80 mm, 1/500, f/10, ISO 1600
© 2005, 2015 by Shawn M. Tomlinson

quietly, in the shadows where no one could see me —
suddenly I could get hundreds of images on a 1gb SD
card.

And, since the ISO would go all the way up to 3200
— 3200 ISO film was rare and expensive, so I never
shot it — I figured that would cover every contingency.

And it did, especially for newspaper work where
the paper is of the worst quality possible. Even though
by then newspapers were printing color photos, it was
hard to see noise on newsprint. So I was content for a
while.

For my own photography, though, I started noticing the noise. A lot.

Still, I wasn't that serious about photography then,

so I just assumed the noise problems were the result of not having a very good camera.

A few years later, SD cards got much cheaper and Pentax offered a free firmware upgrade that allowed the *ist DS to use cards with more capacity than 1gb.

> **I thought, what the hell, I could try this RAW shooting thing. It couldn't hurt.**
>
> **The change was dramatic and amazing.**

I also read a lot more about ISO and realized I needed to cut back a bit. All the way back to 200 ISO.

I thought, what the hell, I could try this RAW shooting thing. It couldn't hurt.

The change was dramatic and amazing.

Suddenly, my not-very-good DSLR was very good. The colors were dramatically better. The sharpness increase was significant, and at 200 ISO there was virtually no noise even in enlargements.

Also by then I had become very deft with Photoshop and Adobe constantly was expanding how the program handled RAW images.

Yes, RAW files will take more room on your memory card and your hard drive. Ansel Adams used an 8-by-10 film camera that was so heavy he had to pack it up mountains on the backs of mules. He only got one shot per film sheet. If he miscalculated, he wouldn't know he had a bad image until he spent hours in the darkroom.

Quality takes sacrifices.

ALWAYS shoot in RAW.

ALWAYS.

And be thankful you are not one of Ansel's assistants who had to carry his equipment when the mules were tired.

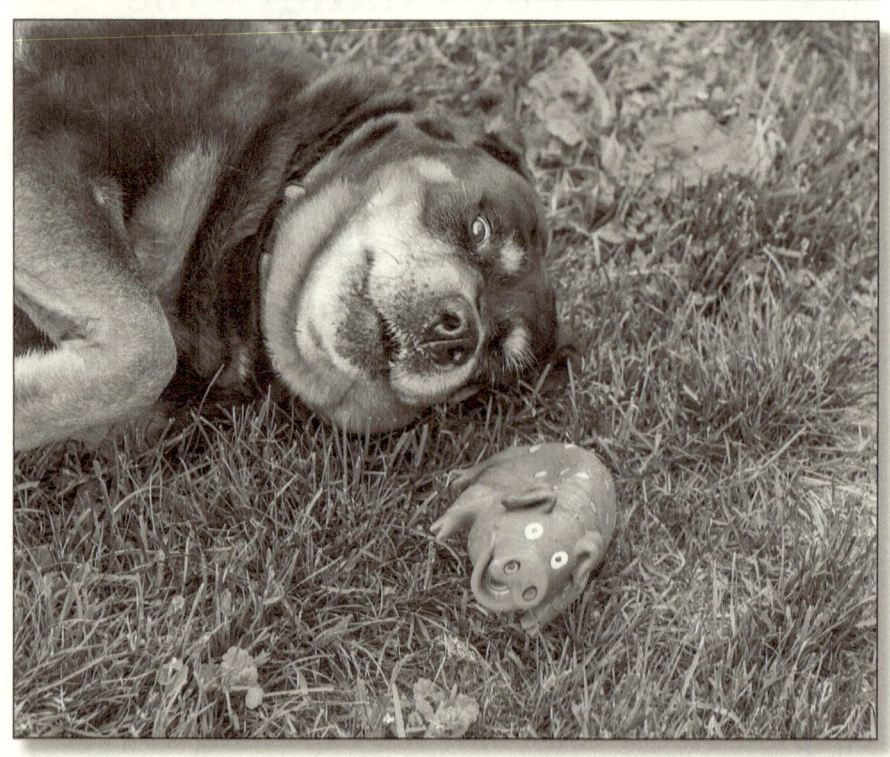

Ballston Lake, N.Y., May 16, 2015.
Canon EOS 20D, 50mm, 1/800, f/3.2, ISO 400, Tv, Pattern Metering
Photo © 2015 by Shawn M. Tomlinson

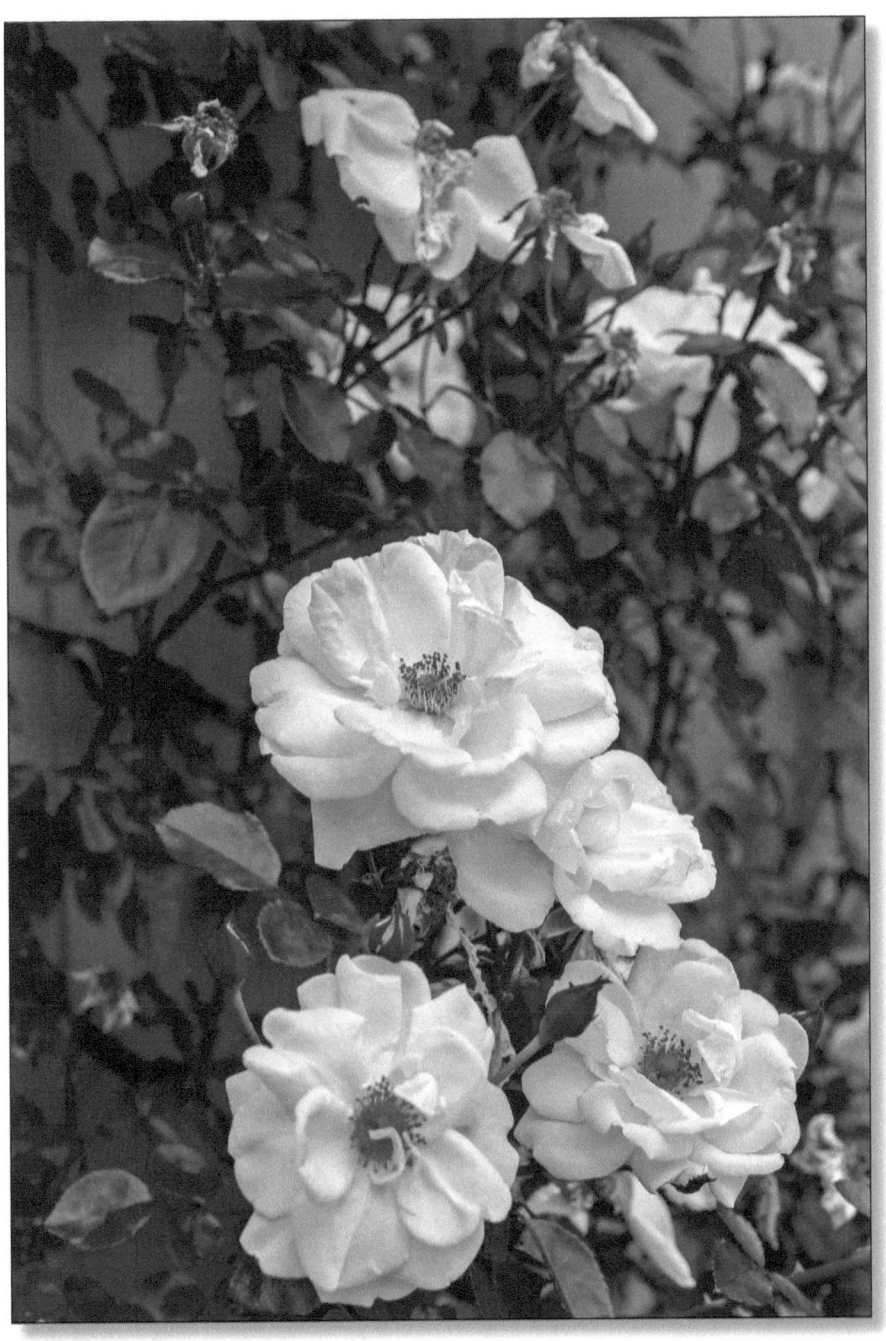

Saratoga Springs, N.Y., June 27, 2015.
Nikon D800e, 50mm, 1/800, f/9, ISO 400, Tv, Pattern Metering
Photo © 2015 by Shawn M. Tomlinson

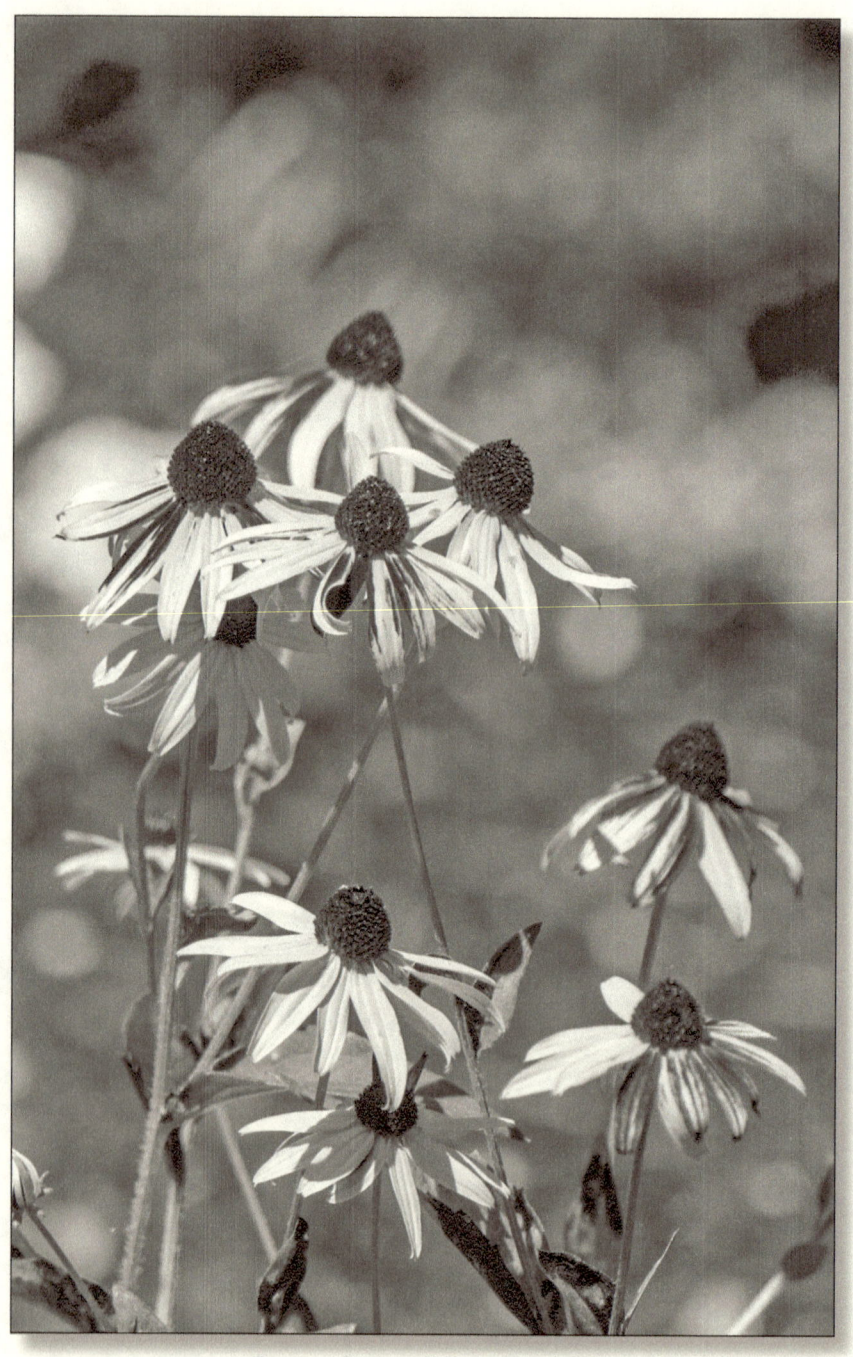

Saratoga Springs, N.Y., Aug. 19, 2014.
Nikon D70 (6.1 megapixels), 300mm, 1/2000, f/6, ISO 250
© 2014, 2015 by Shawn M. Tomlinson

I SO Important

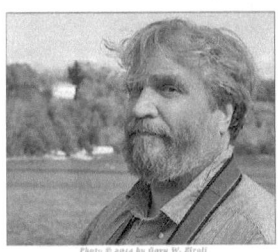

The 12 Steps of Photography

S t e p

3

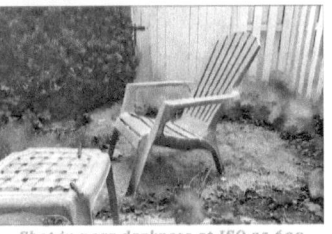

Shot in near darkness at ISO 25,600

Yes, I titled this chapter that.

I really did.

Get the moaning out of the way so we can move on.

Along with shooting ALWAYS in RAW, the other vital component is paying attention to ISO sensitivity.

The higher the ISO, the greater sensitivity there is to light. This means you can shoot in low-light situations, and it means you can use faster shutter speeds. Faster shutter speeds cut down on lens motion blur and give crisper images.

So, then, why wouldn't you want to shoot at high ISO all the time? The camera makers keep raising the ISO sensitivity all the time, so they must want you to use them, right? The Nikon D4S has a top ISO of 204,800, which means it should see through the steel sides of the Titanic in ocean depths, but probably doesn't.

I'm not quite certain why ISO sensitivity keeps increasing in newer cameras. Probably just a selling point. Kai Wong of DigitalRevTV fame, calls these the "stupid ISOs." It is true that picture quality keeps getting more usable at higher ISOs, but I've shot some tests at 25,600 ISO — my Nikon D7000's top stupid ISO — and admittedly it gives some really interesting effects, but not much that's really usable.

Anyway, the things to keep in mind when setting ISO is that the lower — down to 200 ISO — the better for image quality and sharpness. Below 200 ISO and dynamic range usually suffers a bit, and above 400 ISO grain starts to creep in.

There are times you will need to shoot at higher ISO levels, but if you always remember to keep it

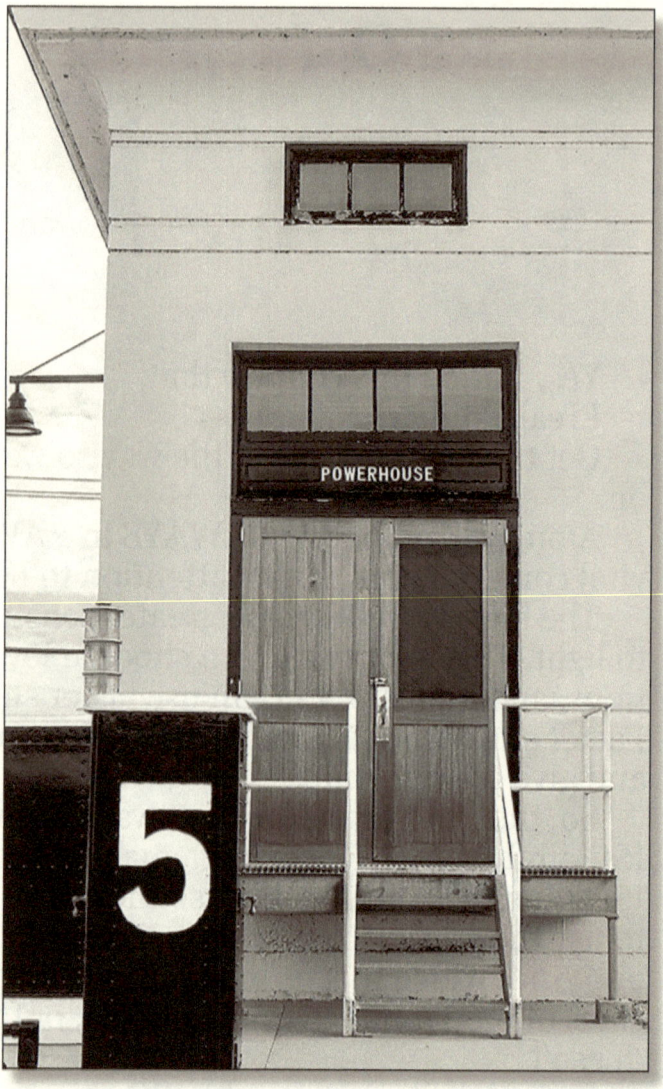

Lock C5, Schuylerville, N.Y., Nov. 8, 2014.
Nikon D7000 (16.2 megapixels), 35 mm (prime), 1/1600, f/3.5, ISO 250
© 2014, 2015 by Shawn M. Tomlinson

the lowest possible for your lighting situation, it will make your images better.

While we are on ISO, this is probably a good place to talk a little about exposure modes, just because I don't want to spend a lot of time on it and most people do what they want to do.

Forget the little pictographs on your Mode Dial. They are for amateurs. They will not usually give great images, but they may stumble upon one once in a while.

The four main exposure modes on most cameras — although Pentax has an extra one — are:

Program
Shutter-Priority
Aperture-Priority
Manual

Think of Program Mode like training wheels on a bicycle. It lets the camera decide upon shutter speed and aperture depending upon the ISO you've set and the light that's hitting the meter. It will give you pretty good images.

But, as training wheels, use the training Program Mode gives you. In most DSLRs, when you compose the image and focus by half-pressing the shutter button, little numbers will pop up in your viewfinder. These numbers will tell two very important things to remember: what shutter speed the DSLR chose and what aperture setting it will use. Looking at these two numbers, taking the photo and then reviewing it on the LCD should start giving you a good idea of how shutter speed and aperture balance and work together.

That's in the field. On the computer screen in virtually any photo-editing software, you can find this same data recorded by the camera at the time of exposure and embedded in the file. In the most common photo editor, Photoshop, go to the File Menu, then to File Info, then to the Camera Data tab. All the information the camera recorded about itself during

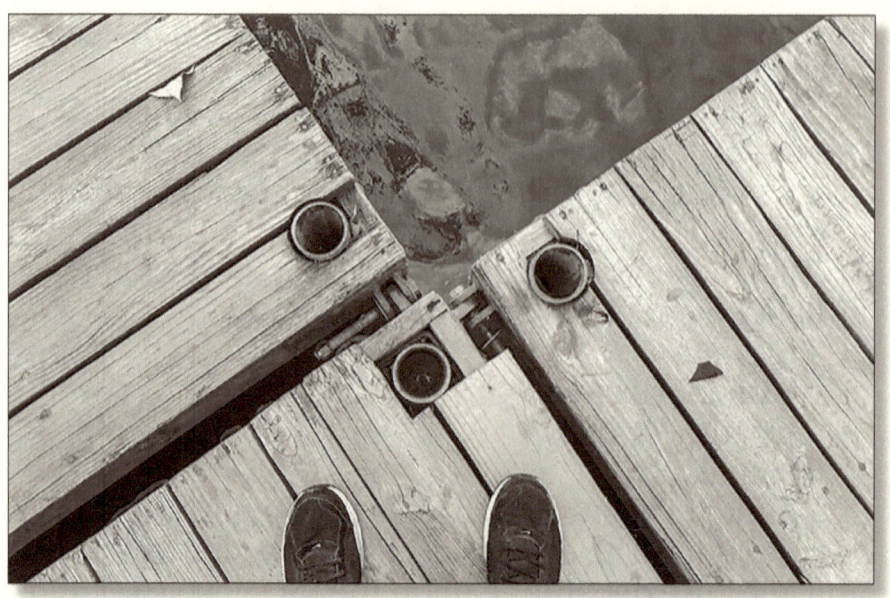

Shawn M. Tomlinson, Gateway Park, Mohawk River, Schenectady, N.Y., Oct. 10, 2014.
Nikon D7000 (16.2 megapixels), 18 mm, 1/640, f/7.1, ISO 400
© 2014, 2015 by Shawn M. Tomlinson

exposure is there.

This information may appear esoteric and mystifying at first, but gradually, you will associate the numbers with what you see on the screen of the camera and computer.

As always, though, we grow up. The training wheels can't stay on forever. It's time to take control of one aspect of the exposure, either the shutter speed or the aperture. Once you've chosen on, the DSLR still will help you along by choosing the other.

Shutter-Priority Mode, signified on the Mode Dial by Tv for some reason, allows you to choose the shutter speed. For example, and taking the bicycle motif way too far, let's say you want to photograph your daughter as her training wheels have just come off and she wants to show off her new skills. She's not a race car driver, but she will be moving. To keep her from blurring and to "freeze" her motion as she rides, you will want a higher shutter speed. If Program Mode would have chosen 1/320 of a second, you may want to choose 1/1000.

Program Mode chose 1/320 of a second to balance with a medium-range aperture f-stop, probably around f/5.6 or f/8 depending upon the light. However, 1/320 may not be fast enough to stop the cyclist from blurring. 1/1000 will. So, when you use Shutter-Priority Mode, you select 1/1000 and the DSLR brain will accommodate you by opening the aperture to f/3.5 or f/2.8 or bigger, if you lens will do it.

It works just the opposite with Aperture-Priority Mode (Av on your dial) in that you select the aperture and the DSLR sets the shutter speed. There are many reasons to do this, but the one most beginners want to try — and I like it myself — is increasing depth-of-field.

Depth-of-Field is the measure of how things at different distances in your viewfinder will be in focus. If you shoot with your lens wide open, such as a 50mm lens at f/1.8, you only get a shallow depth-of-field, meaning only what you focus upon will be in focus. Objects in front of or behind your subject will blur. This is a useful effect known as bokeh.

However, if you want the dog in the foreground, your daughter riding her bike in the middle and her mother waving her on in the background all to be relatively sharp and in focus, you need to "stop-down" the lens to a smaller aperture. The smaller the aperture, the more things at different distances will be discernible. However, beyond f/22 or so, things get fuzzy again.

So, OK, you want the dog, the girl and her mother in focus, so set the aperture at f/11. As you push the shutter button halfway to focus, the DSLR selects the appropriate shutter speed to get a good exposure for you. Some DSLRs — especially higher end cameras — have a depth-of-field preview button to give you a sense of what will be in focus at different aperture settings before you make the exposure.

Once these additional training wheels are off — yes, you're riding a unicycle by now — it's down to Manual Mode. This is the goal of every photographer: the knowledge and experience to understand the light in any condition and select the shutter speed and aperture based upon that without the DSLR brain thinking it's smarter than you.

All of these Modes are based upon the ISO sensitivity you set. See how we came full-circle to that? The DSLR uses the ISO setting to make its adjustments

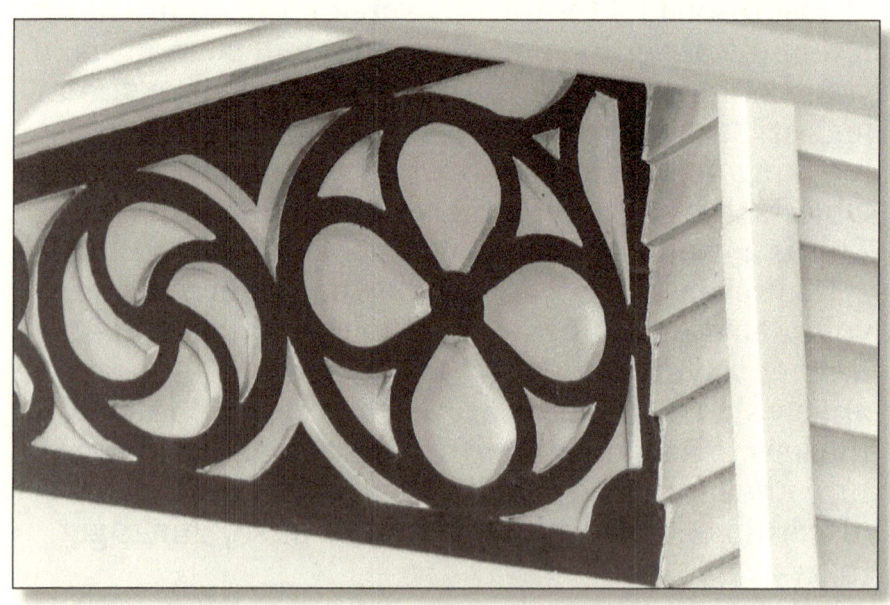

Saratoga Springs, N.Y., Aug. 30, 2014.
Nikon D70 (6.1 megapixels), 190mm, 1/200, f/4.8, ISO 400
© 2014, 2015 by Shawn M. Tomlinson

in Program, Shutter-Priority and Aperture-Priority Modes. You will use it yourself when you move to Manual Mode.

There's no rush, though.

The more you shoot in the other Modes, the more you will learn toward the ultimate goal of Manual Mode.

Oh, and, of course, the best way to find out for yourself how all this works together is to go out and shoot test images. Set up your DSLR on a tripod. Shoot the scene in Program. Then move to Tv and try different shutter speeds. Then to Av and try different apertures.

Then to Manual and mix-and-match settings. It costs nothing but your time to make these tests for yourself and, because the exposure data is recorded for each file, you can compare your images later to see which ones worked best at which settings combination.

The keys to becoming a good photographer are experimentation and persistence. Unlike with film — where every roll you shot cost twice: to buy then to develop — in digital, it just takes reformatting the memory card to start all over again.

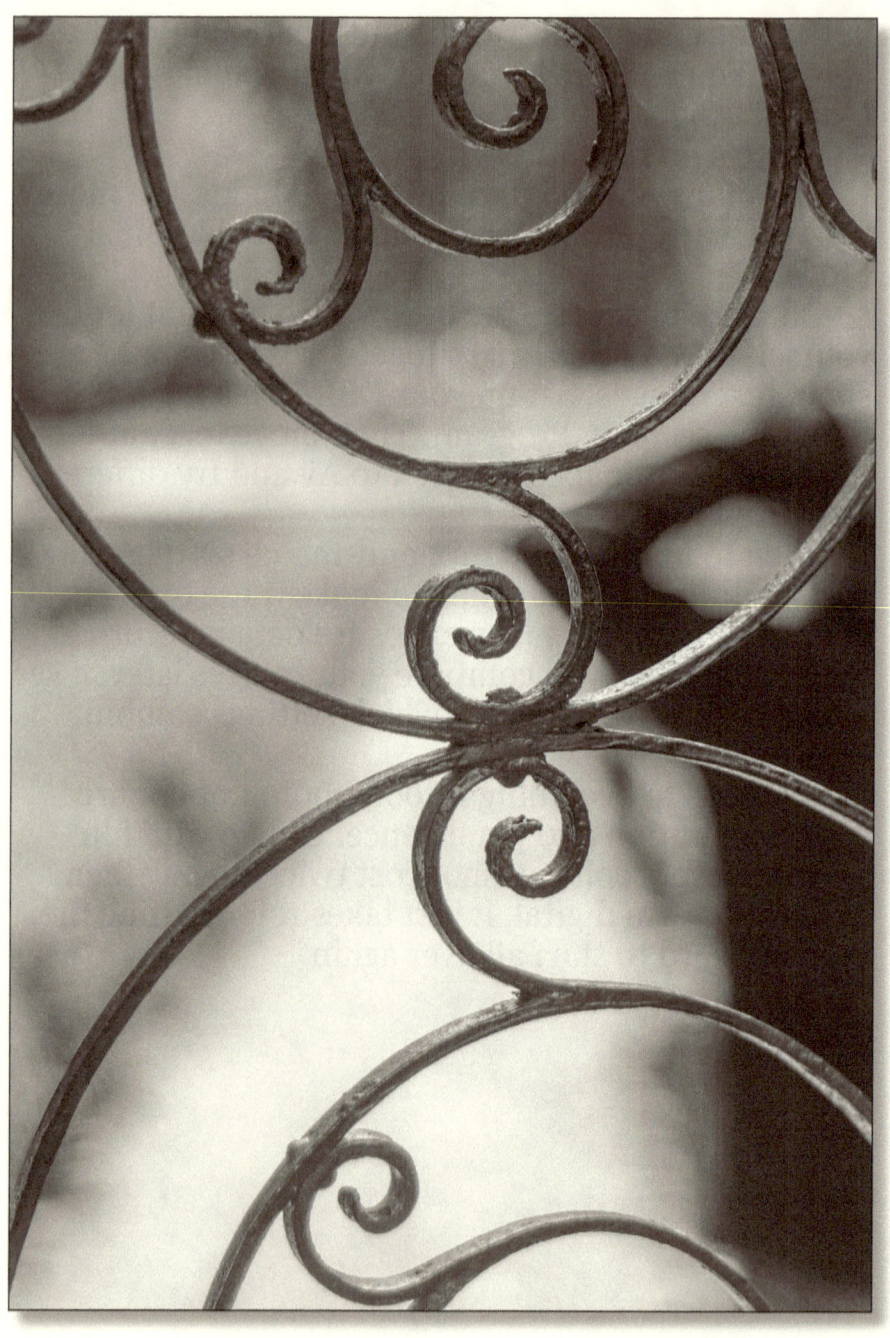

Gary W. Ziroli, Yaddo, Saratoga Springs, N.Y., May 23, 2015.
Nikon D7000, 50mm, 1/2500, f/2.5, ISO 200, Tv, Pattern Metering
Photo © 2015 by Shawn M. Tomlinson

Shoot

The 12 Steps of Photography

Step 4

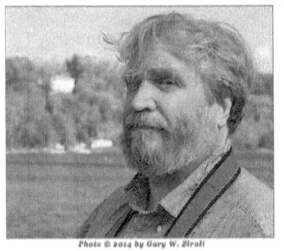

Photo © 2014 by Gary W. Ziroli

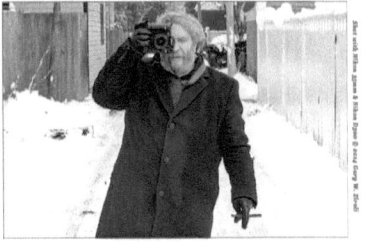

Nothing is more important then simply shooting photographs for a photographer.

It's more important than having the best equipment.

It's more important than developing photo-editing skills.

It's more important than waiting to get the funds to take a trip to the Grand Canyon to shoot.

Just shoot.

And then shoot some more.

All the tipsters who write columns and articles giving you tips about your photographic technique usually mention that you should, ah, ya know, occasionally shoot some photographs. They may have various deep-breathing exercises or Yoga techniques or meditation mantras for you to repeat, and frankly, anything that works is a good thing.

Here's what I do.

I shoot every day.

Not just some days.

Not just when I'm going someplace cool.

Not just when the mood takes me.

Every.

Day.

OK, I hear you say that you've got jobs and families and soccer matches and PTA meetings and the gym and everything else.

Just excuses.

If you are serious about being a photographer, these are just excuses.

Oh, I believe you have all these constant activities. No question.

You still must find time to shoot every single day.

You don't even have to shoot for long each day, although, of course, whenever you can, shoot for as long a period as possible.

I set two or three days each week to go on what I call (and nicked from the Lewis & Clark Expedition) "Voyage of Photography." These are longer sessions in which I go to locations or walk around villages or cities, or something else planned.

The other days of the week, in between everything else I must do, I make a time first in my head, then adjust it for reality, to grab the DSLR and head out the door. Sometimes, these sessions last an hour or two,

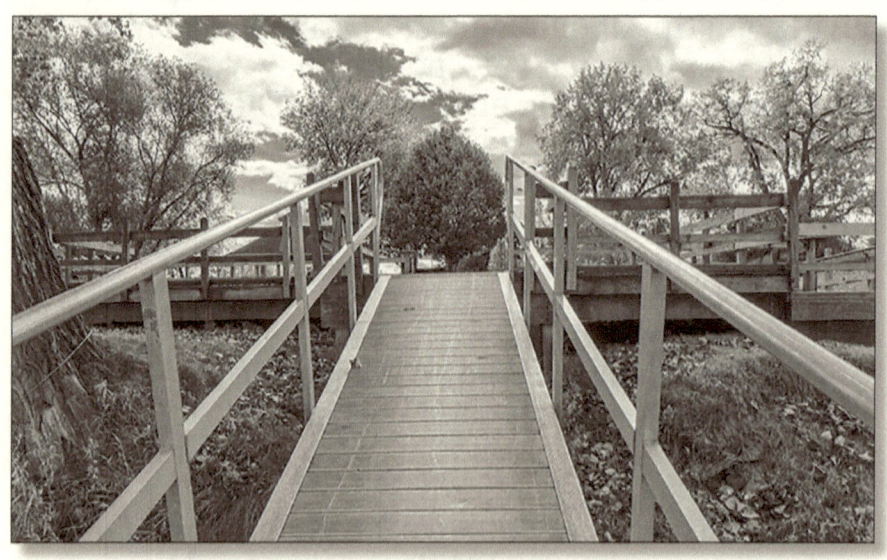

Gateway Park, Mohawk River, Schenectady, N.Y., Oct. 10, 2014.
Nikon D7000 (16.2 megapixels), 18 mm, 1/640, f/10, ISO 400
© 2014, 2015 by Shawn M. Tomlinson

but more frequently, 20 or 30 minutes.

Like those people trying to sell you on exercise and exercise equipment say, certainly you can find 20 to 30 minutes to workout your photographic muscles. And, you don't need days in between your sessions to rest these muscles.

Which brings up the whiny questions, "What can I shoot? Where can I go? I live in Iowa. There's nothing interesting to photograph. Wah!"

OK, I can't do anything about the Iowa thing. I once turned down a job offer from a friend to write

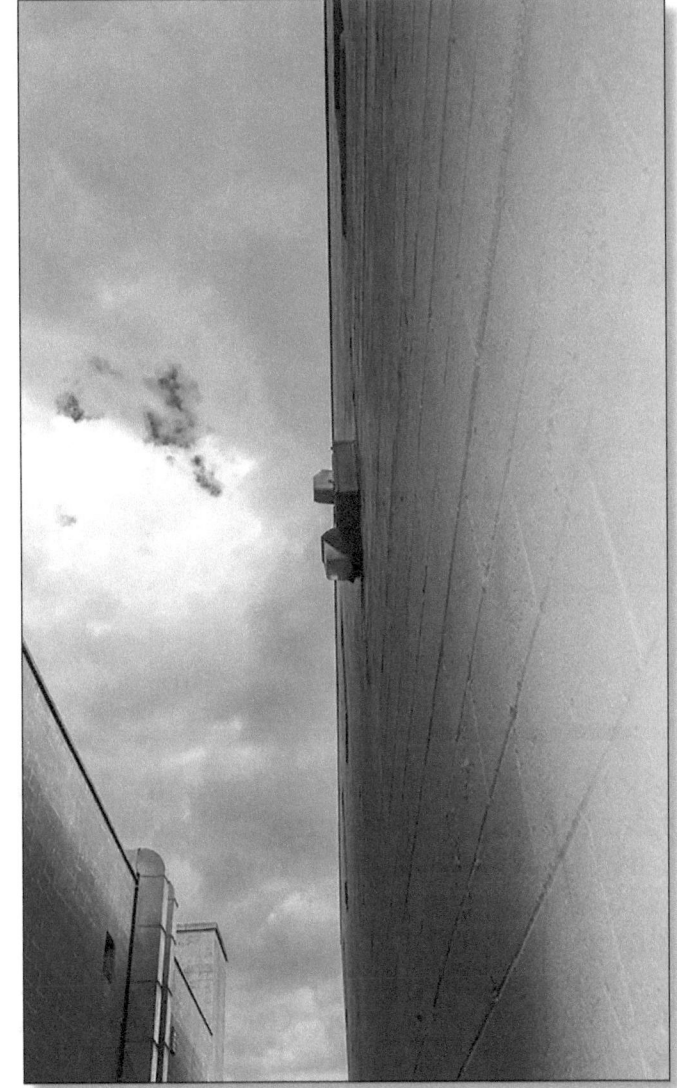

Saratoga Springs, N.Y., Oct. 11, 2014.
Nikon D7000 (16.2 megapixels), 18 mm, 1/250, f/13, ISO 400
© 2014, 2015 by Shawn M. Tomlinson

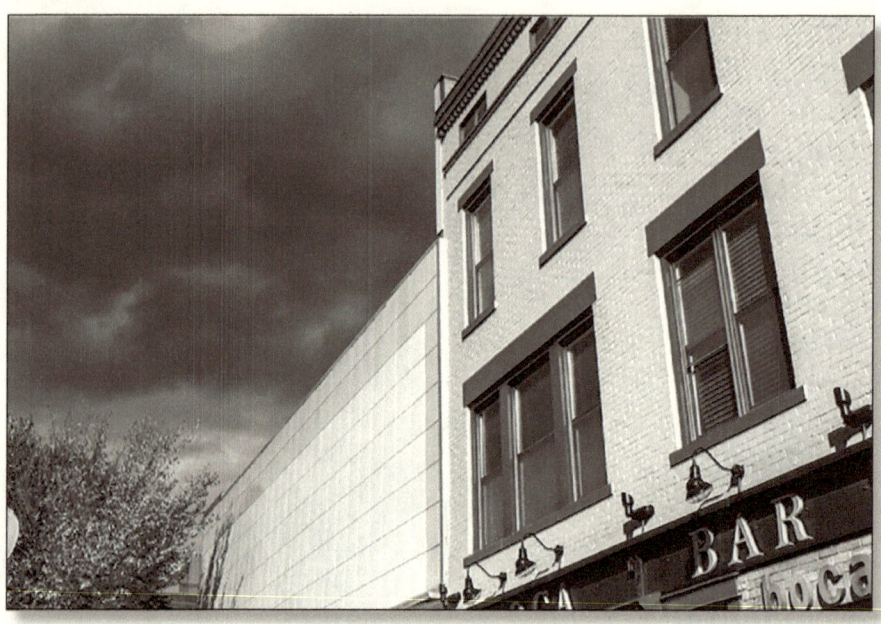

Saratoga Springs, N.Y., Oct. 11, 2014.
Nikon D7000 (16.2 megapixels), 26 mm, 1/500, f/14, ISO 400
© 2014, 2015 by Shawn M. Tomlinson

about Apple and Macs in Iowa just because I couldn't bear the thought of being and living there. But, God forbid, if I had to go to Iowa or anyplace else in the Mid-Waste again, I'll bet I could find interesting things to photograph every single day.

You can look at maps to find interesting locations not that far away. With Google Earth, you also can get an vague idea at least of what the place looks like before you get there. Yes, I said before you get there because your looking at the maps on your home computer because you already smashed or voluntarily gave up your smartphone.

I have found wonderful places not 10 miles from where I live that I never knew were there. For example, one of my favorite places to go to for a Voyage of Photography session is called the Stockade in Schenectady. This is the oldest part of the city and now is home to one of the nicer neighborhoods of a depressed city. The old houses, the narrow streets, etc., are great to photograph. I knew the Stockade bordered the Mohawk River, but I had photographed the neighborhood many times before I ventured down one of the streets toward the river. To my surprise, there was a park there. It's a long, narrow park that borders the river, cleverly called Riverside Park. I've gotten some great images there.

Another example. I was looking at Google Earth at the same river upstream and notices some white water in the satellite image. It turned out to be a hydroelectric dam with one of the modern canal locks on the other side. Just up river from there, I saw the old locks and even the remains of a dry dock for the old Erie or Champlain canals. I'd never been to any of

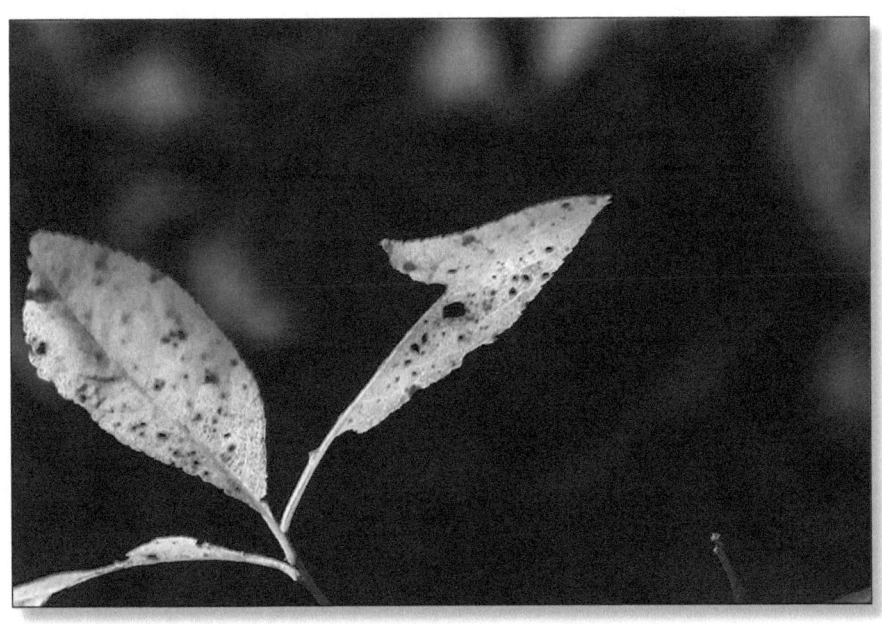

Ballston Lake, N.Y., Nov. 2, 2014.
Nikon D7000 (16.2 megapixels), 300 mm, 1/1000, f/5.6, ISO 400
© 2014, 2015 by Shawn M. Tomlinson

these places, so I got in the car and over several days, shot more than 2,500 images there.

Those types of photo shoots take some time and you don't have any. You're squeezing out those 20 to 30 minutes.

I know it sounds dull and stupid. I do. But believe me, it isn't.

Just step outside your door.

Yes, I know.

All the high-priced photography seminars and workshops generally say to go to Machu Picchu or Atlantis or wherever. That would be great, but probably not doable in 20 to 30 minutes.

I had started shooting around my house already, but then I broke my foot — not while being a photographer, but while being a garage cleaner to get my car inside for the winter — and suddenly walking out in the front yard or backyard was a struggle enough without even thinking about getting to the Angkor Wat or hopping in my TARDIS to photograph the Hanging Gardens of Babylon.

Because I refused to go to the doctor for two weeks, I was walking on the broken foot and that meant I could only walk a little. So, the surroundings of my small suburban house, dull by most standards — especially in the winter when this happened — suddenly became my main venue. It was only four weeks after the foot-breaking incident that I started my shoot-every-day-no-matter-what creed.

My house has a fenced-in backyard, a rottwieller, a lot of flowers and multi-colored leaves, a weather-worn deck, and a wetland beyond the fence. In the front is a dying old tree, a birdbath and birdhouse, a headless goose statue, more flowers, red winter berries, a cracked sidewalk and a crazy felon living across the street.

Just exploring this small area in all kinds of light — morning, afternoon, evening, winter, summer, spring, autumn, etc. — has captured for me thousands of photographs, many of them quite good.

It doesn't matter if you lack a yard. No matter where you live, you have to walk outside at some point during the day. It's all become routine, I know, but if you really look, there are endless photographic subjects within reach. You may find you become very good at certain subjects you never thought would interest you. For example, I always liked flowers, but at just about the same level most people do. I barely noticed them and once in a while said, "Ooo, that's pretty" and moved on.

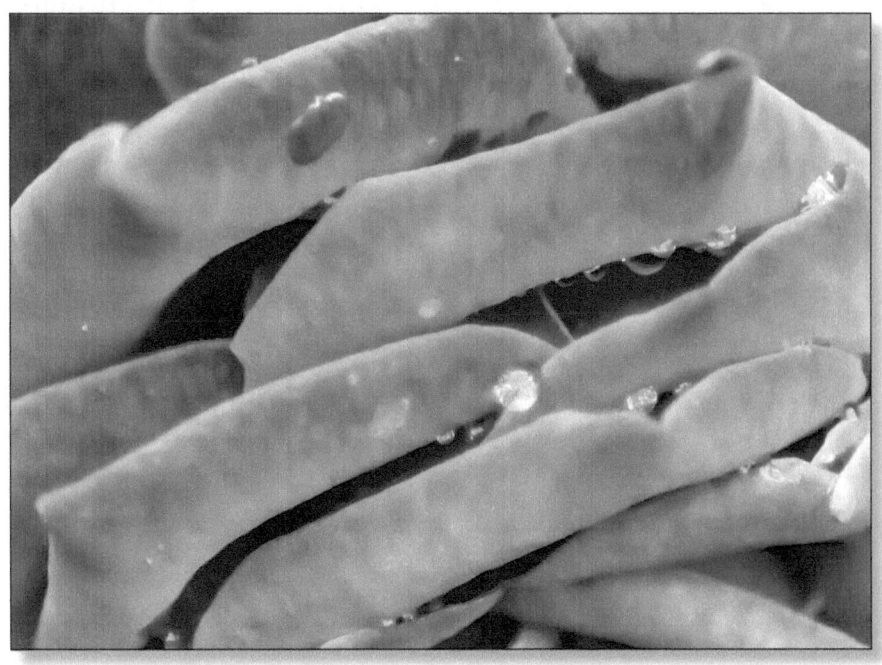

Rose Garden, Central Park, Schenectady, N.Y., Aug. 17, 2014.
Nikon D70 (6.1 megapixels), 300mm, 1/400, f/6, ISO 400
© 2014, 2015 by Shawn M. Tomlinson

Then I got a Tamron 70-300mm lens used for $29, mounted it to first my Nikon D1, then the Nikon D70, then the Nikon D7000 (all old cameras by now, especially the D1, which was marketed in the last century). Suddenly, because of the bokeh, I got very interested in flowers.

Again, looking at a map, I discovered there is a rose garden in Schenectady's Central Park. I jumped in the car — it was July by then and the foot was healed — with the D1 and D70 (I didn't have the fantastic D7000 yet) and spent a couple of hours shooting nothing but flowers and the surroundings of the rose garden, including a great fountain. I took the best flower images I've ever done, learned a lot in the process, and produced a photo eBook of the voyage.

Apart from all the other points here, the 70-300mm lens was on the Nikon D70, which only has 6.1 megapixels for resolution. And many of the images were astonishing. You don't need mega megapixels to do great work.

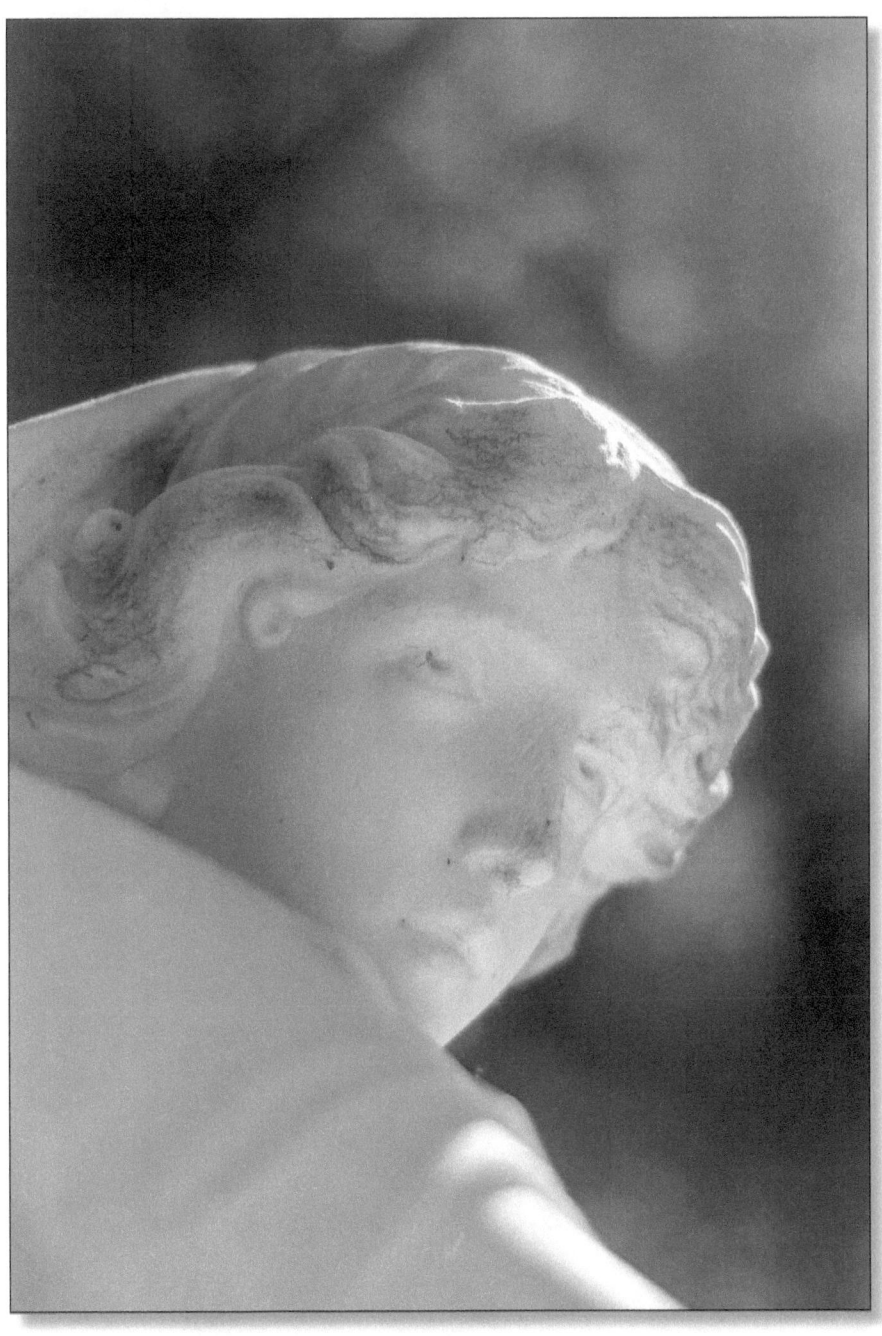

Yaddo, Saratoga Springs, N.Y., May 23, 2015.
Nikon D7000, 50mm, 1/5000, f/2, ISO 200, Tv, Pattern Metering
Photo © 2015 by Shawn M. Tomlinson

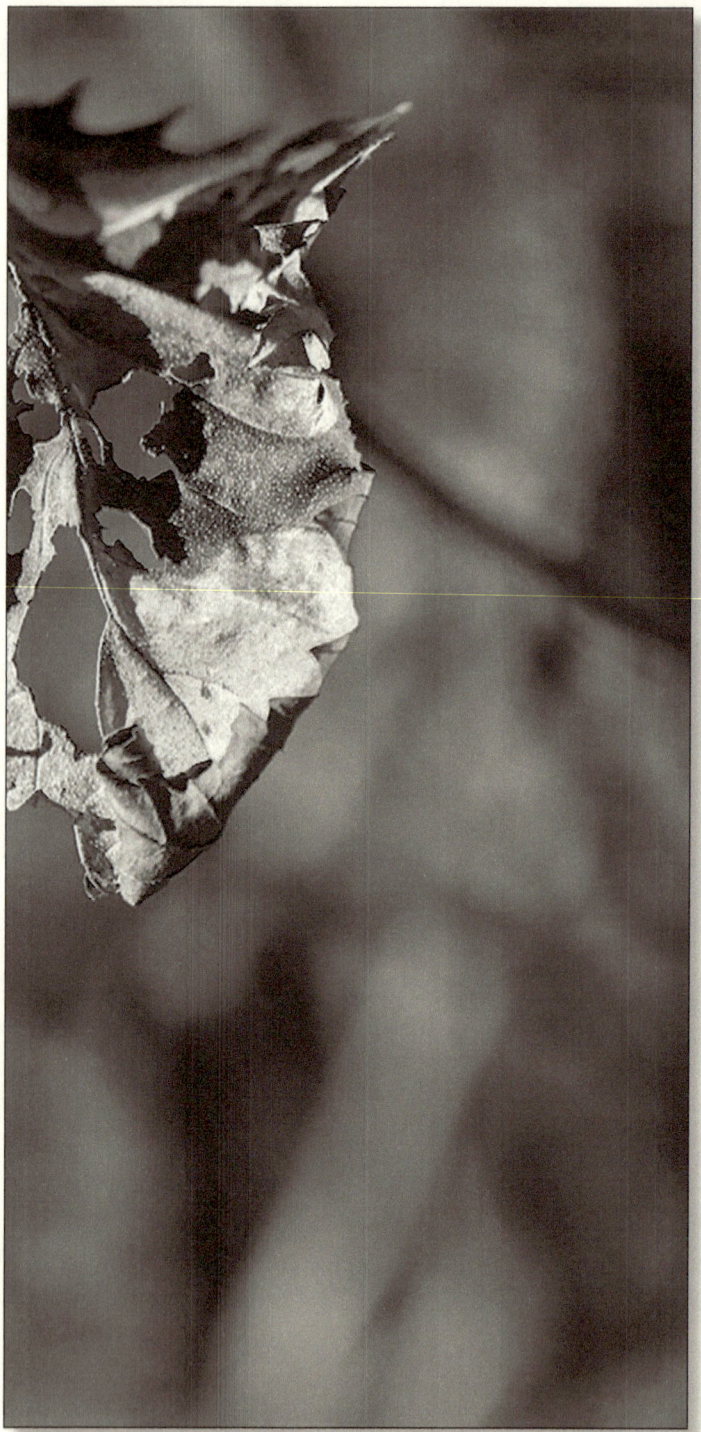

Ballston Lake,
N.Y.,
Nov. 2,
2014.

Nikon
D7000
(16.2 mp),
180 mm, 1/1000,
f/8,
ISO 400

© 2014, 2015
shawn m
tomlinson

Keep Shooting

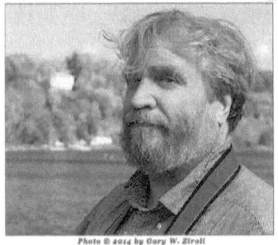

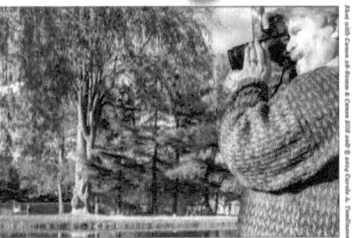

Photo © 2014 by Gary W. Ziroli

In case I haven't stressed it enough, keep shooting.

I mentioned that I shoot fantastic images with a $69 6.1-megapixel Nikon D70 and a $29 Tamron 70-300mm zoom lens. I mentioned this specifically because at this point along the way of these tips, it makes some senses to talk about getting the best equipment possible for the least amount of money.

As I may have indicated, I — and most likely you — would love to acquire each new-and-nifty DSLR that comes out and the best and most expensive lenses. It is rare that a photographer has that kind of financing, so even most pros don't get every camera body, lens or accessory they want. They get what is practical, what they need, what is most likely to make them money.

Unless you are a pro already, you probably drool over all the latest stuff like most photographers do, but even though the scale will be smaller in most cases, the basic philosophy of the pros — or part of it — should govern the equipment you buy: what is practical and what you need.

The simplest way to get started and the one most likely to keep you shooting — again, the single most important thing here — is to buy an older model DSLR and an 18-200mm "travel" lens to go with it. This is not the best setup, but it is the best to start.

So, to get started with that constant shooting thing I keep on about, here are some suggestions for DSLR bodies. Keep in mind that this list is made with the consideration that you want to start shooting with a DSLR but either can't or don't want to lay out the bucks for a spanking brand new one. This actually can be a good thing. It gets you started sooner, and if you are willing to buy older, used equipment from a reputable dealer, you can get a higher-level DSLR than you could get with more money for a new entry-level camera.

DSLRs are broken roughly into three levels with some in-betweener levels occasionally thrown in.

Entry Level

The basic, lowest-end, least expensive DSLR. It is made chiefly of plastic and feels it. It won't take much of a beating and it won't have that neat-o info LCD on the top right of the camera body. These may have high resolution — many of them do now — but it isn't much use without a top quality lens that pushes the price way up.

The models here are current as of late 2014, but will change often. However, not much does change on them and they tend to look roughly the same as the previous model. The designations camera makers give them do not always follow logical patterns, so probably the best way to determine if that camera you're holding tethered to the counter at Best Buy is the lowest entry level DSLR is the price.

Canon has three low-end DSLRs at the moment:
• EOS Rebel T3i
• EOS Rebel T5
• EOS Rebel T3

These range in price new from $450 to $600, each with the kit 18-55mm lens. The one downside of buying an entry-level DSLR from Canon in the United States is that you bear the mark of the "REBEL" on the front of your camera like the red "A" Hester Prin is forced to wear in Nathaniel Hawthorne's The Scarlet Letter. If you live elsewhere the same cameras have numerical designations rather than the embarrassing "REBEL" on the front.

The EOS Rebel T3i is the top of Canon's entry-level group with 18 megapixels and a tilty-flippy LCD. The

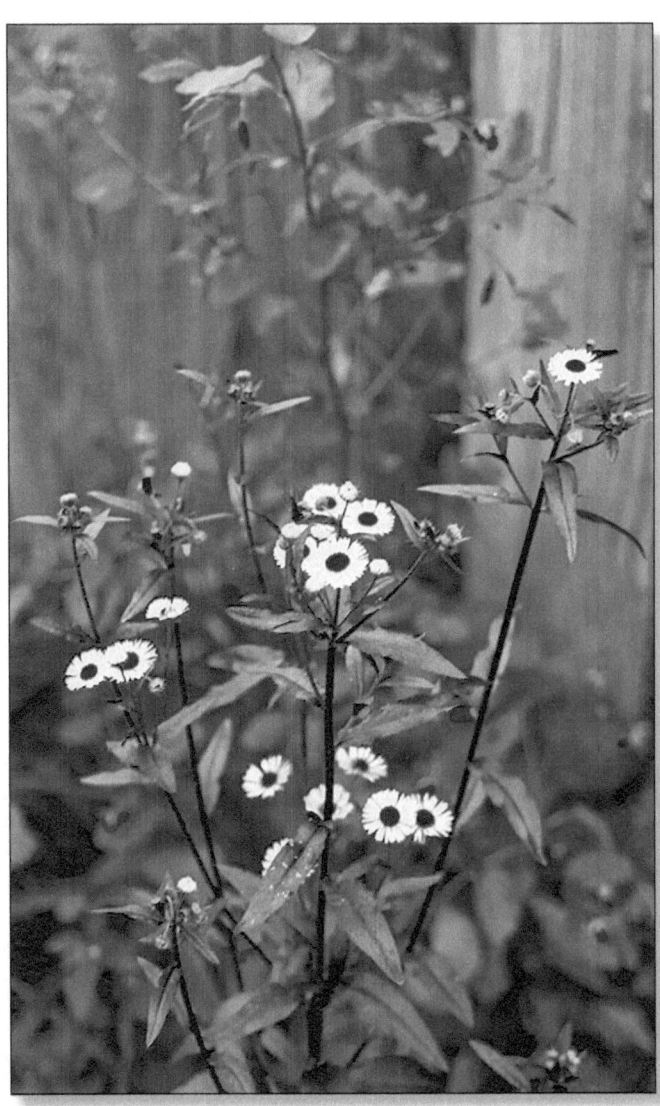

Ballston Lake, N.Y., Sept. 8, 2014.
Canon EOS 1DS (11.1 megapixels), 80 mm, 1/60, f/5.6, ISO 400
© 2014, 2015 by Shawn M. Tomlinson

middle T5, also at 18 megapixels, and for $50 less does not have the tilty screen thingy. The T3 sports a 12.2-megapixel sensor. Megapixels don't mean all that much. See part 6 for an explanation of that.

Nikon has two low-end DSRLs without very little difference between them except price:
• D5300
• D3300
The main difference between these two 24-megapixel DSLRs is that the D5300 has a tilty-flippy screen and the D3300 doesn't. The D5300 lists for $700 and the D3300 has a retail price of $500. At those prices, neither comes with a lens.

Pentax recently introduced a really silly looking

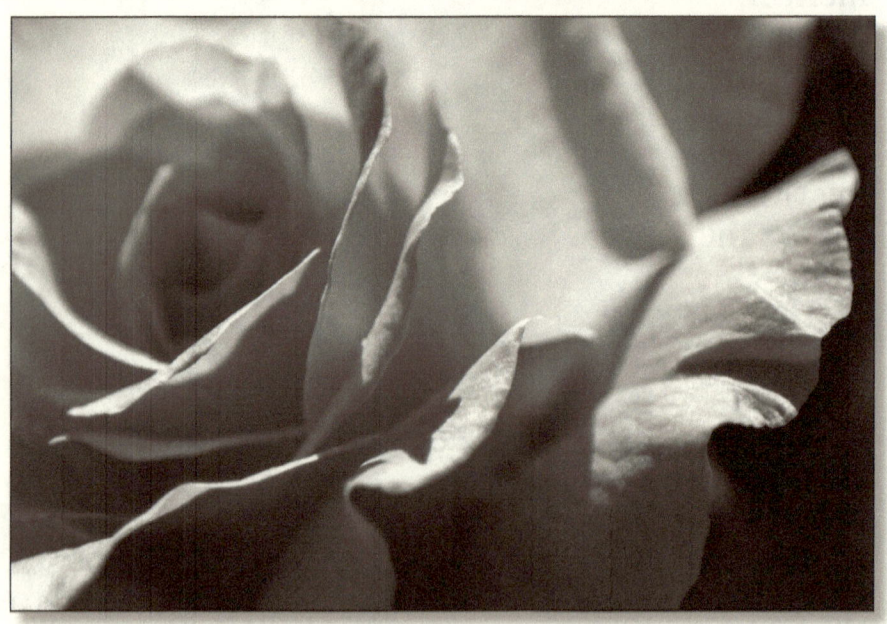

Rose Garden, Central Park, Schenectady, N.Y., Aug. 17, 2014.
Nikon D70 (6.1 megapixels), 270mm, 1/4000, f/5.6, ISO 250
© 2014, 2015 by Shawn M. Tomlinson

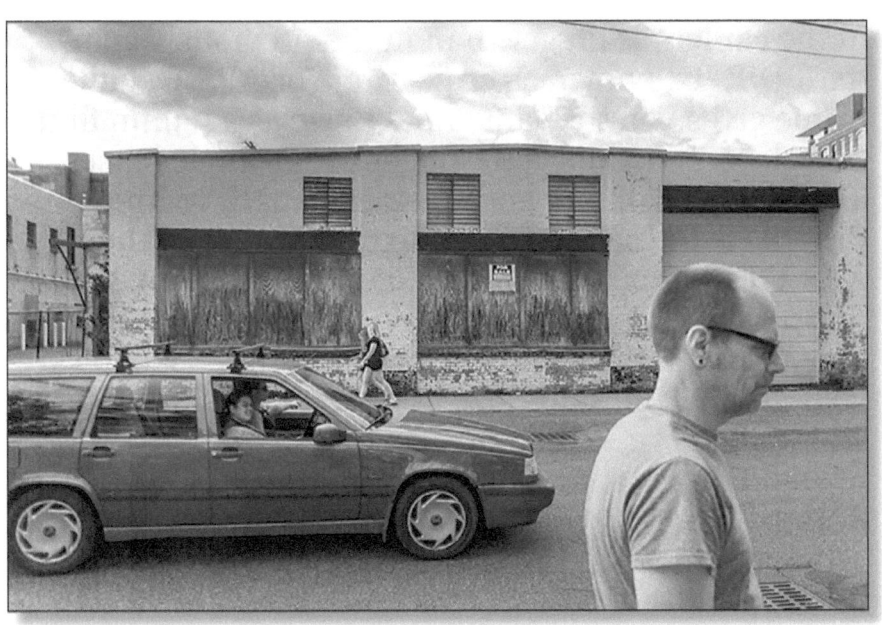

Gary Ziroli, Saratoga Springs, N.Y., Aug. 9, 2014.
Pentax K20D (14.2 megapixels), 18 mm, 1/500, f/4.5, ISO 280
© 2014, 2015 by Shawn M. Tomlinson

line of multi-colored DSLRs, but it keeps selling the main, respectable low-end K-50 for a very low price of $400. The K-50 also comes in a variety of colors, but without the flashy lights.

Sony still makes a few non-mirrorless DSLRs, but nothing one could call entry-level.

The next level up is the enthusiast or advanced amateur level. DSLRs in this range are typically better built with more pro-like features.

Canon has the 70D, Nikon the D7100, Pentax the K-5 II.

At the semi-pro level, all but Pentax have moved to full-frame DSLRs. Full frame means that the sensor of the camera is bigger than in the previously standard DSLRs, known as crop-frame or APS-C. Full frame gives you the same image size as a 35mm film SLR does. It means you can get wider-angle lenses for a full-frame camera, and the focal length written on the lens is the actual focal length. Because of the way APS-C cameras work, Nikon, Pentax and Sony have a "crop factor" of 1.5x and Canon as one of 1.6x. So, OK, if a 50mm lens is standard on full frame — it shows your subject the same size as it would be through your naked eye — then on a Nikon, Pentax or Sony, it would be a 75mm, and on a Canon APS-C camera, 80mm.

So, the move in the semi-pro and pro DSLRs is toward full frame.

Canon's semi-pro DSLRs are the Canon EOS 5D Mark III and EOS 6D.

Nikon has its D610, D810 and D750 in this range.

Pentax makes its top-of-the-line K-3 in this range, and does not have a pro DSLR. The K-3 is an APS-C DSLR.

At the top, Canon finally merged its pro APS-C and full-frame camera lines into one, the full-frame EOS 1DX. It's fast, it's sleek and it's $6,800.

Nikon has this weird thing going on with its pro DSLRs. It still makes the older 24-megapixel D3x, but names as it's top camera the 16-megapixel D4S. To make things more confusing, the older D3x costs $8,000 and the newer D4S, $6,500. Go figure.

Any, this is all to show the current lineups and the high prices. If you can afford it, the higher level of DSLR always is better because they are built better. That is, higher level, not necessarily higher price.

So, OK, now that I've scared you enough with new DSLR prices, let's get down to what is practical and what you need.

You don't need 24 megapixels. They are nice, but unless you plan to enlarge your images to billboard size, completely unnecessary.

Most people rarely enlarge their images in print more than 8.5-by-11 inches, and very few even print them anymore.

Which is why most people who have used DSLRs of all ranges say the same thing: You don't really need more

Dance Museum, Saratoga Springs, N.Y., Aug. 5, 2014.
Canon EOS 20D (8.2 megapixels), 37 mm, 1/500, f/14, ISO 400
© 2014, 2015 by Shawn M. Tomlinson

than 6 megapixels for great images. Beyond about 12 megapixels, it really starts to get pointless.

Case in point. My friend and photographic colleague, Gary W. Ziroli, bought a Nikon D300, the last of the semi-pro APS-C cameras from Nikon. He loved it, but thought that, maybe 24-megapixels really would be better. So, he opted for a used Nikon D3200 with its 24 megapixels.

He had it for a couple of weeks. He and I both experimented with it. We don't shoot lab tests, of course, so in the real world, we didn't see much of a difference in the images.

We both saw a very real difference in the "feel" of the cameras. The semi-pro D300 is solid, built well, designed for rugged use.

The D3200 was not. It was mostly plastic and felt

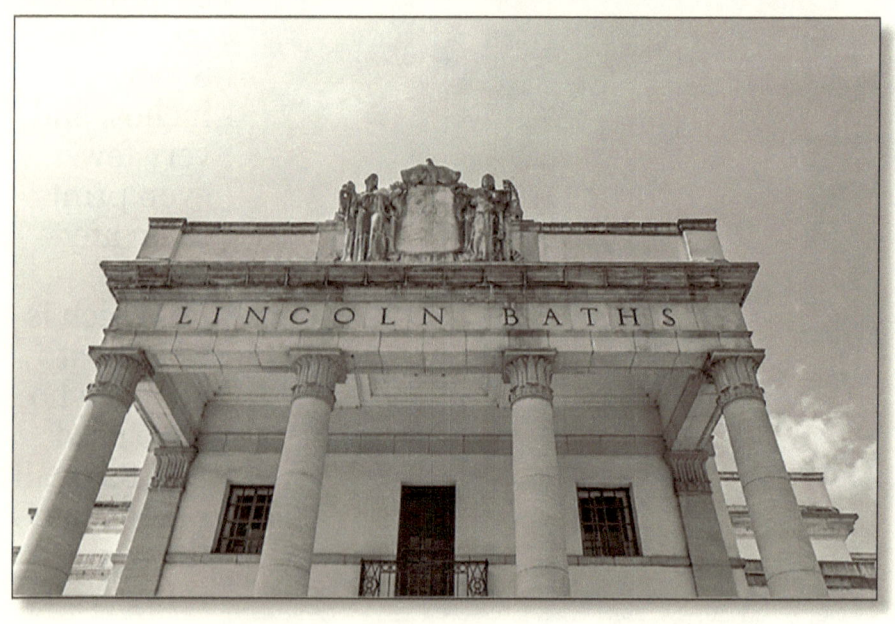

Lincoln Baths, Saratoga Springs, N.Y., Sept. 7, 2014.
Nikon D1 (2.65 megapixels), 18 mm, 1/1250, f/5.6, ISO 200
© 2014, 2015 by Shawn M. Tomlinson

as though it could break relatively easily.

He sent the D3200 back and is quite content with his 12.2 megapixels.

We both also are content with our "ancient" DSLRs. I have the original Nikon D1 and he has its successor, the D1X. The D1 has 2.65 megapixels and the D1X has 5.47 megapixels.

We both get great color and professional images from these cameras.

It doesn't seem possible, but it's true. Despite these low resolution ratings, these are professional DSLRs and much better than, say a 3-megapixel point-and-shoot.

I'm not recommended these or the D1H because they are ancient and quite difficult to use until you learn a lot of stuff.

In fact, I learned just enough of the esoteric codes on the D1 to do what I need and shirked my responsibility and didn't learn the rest.

Great camera, but not as user friendly as one would like.

Anyway, as for the DSLRs I am recommending, well, these are great cameras and produce fantastic images.

From Canon, definitely recommended is the EOS 20D. It is a workhorse, fast and sleek. It can use the modern "digital" lenses unlike it's predecessor, the much-loved EOS 10D.

This is the main reason to get a 20D over a 10D. I've had both and although the 10D is slower, it produces such wonderful color, I miss mine terribly.

I use the 20D quite a bit. You can get one used for around $100. It has 8.2 megapixels.

From Nikon, no question, the D70. The D80 and D90 are a bit better, but they cost a lot more.

You can get a D70 in great shape for around $75. It has 6.1 megapixels.

From Pentax, I would recommend the *ist DS over the *ist D and *ist DL. And yes, those are stupid names, almost as bad as "Rebel."

But the Pentax *ist DS — my first DSLR back in 2005 — is capable of great images. I know. I've shot many with it. It costs around $100 and has 6.1 megapixels.

The Sony A100 with 10.2 megapixels entered the fray later.

I don't own one, but would like to.

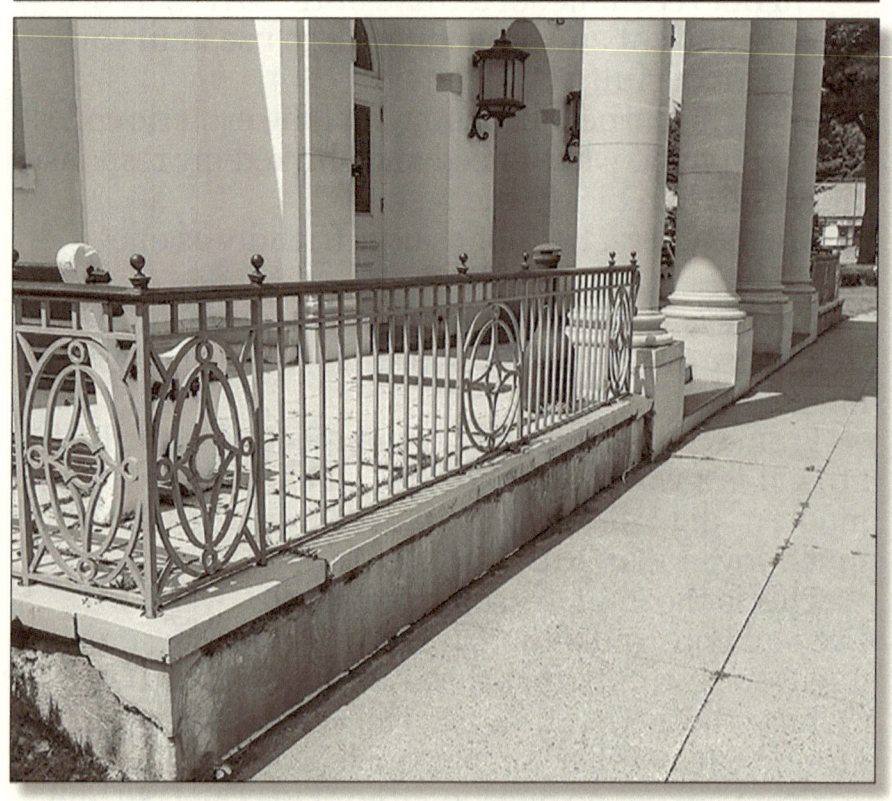

Lincoln Baths, Saratoga Springs, N.Y., Sept. 7, 2014.
Nikon D1 (2.65 megapixels), 18 mm, 1/1250, f/5.6, ISO 200
© 2014, 2015 by Shawn M. Tomlinson

The sample images I've seen make me believe it will give me great images. It costs around $110.

OK, so with one of those cameras in hand, the next thing is the lens.

There are many possibilities, and I'll get into some of them later, but for now, to start, let's only consider the "travel" super zooms.

The advantage to this type of lens is that it covers everything from 18mm to 200mm in one lens.

That's the equivalent of 27-300mm on the Nikon, Pentax and Sony, and 28.2-320mm on the Canon.

It almost always is better to buy lenses from the manufacturer of your camera. Get a Nikon lens for a Nikon DSLR, etc. However, these usually are expensive, and these travel lenses are very good from third-parties, particularly Sigma and Tamron.

Skip the Velveeta (Quantaray; "Quantaray is to lenses as Velveeta is to cheese") and other brands.

Sigma and Tamron make 18-200mm lenses for Canon, Nikon, Pentax and Sony. Tamron lenses range from $100 to $150 used. Sigma, from $120 to $200. The actual brand-name lenses, used, go for:

Canon: $200-$300
Nikon: $260-$500
Pentax: $300-$400
Sony: $170-250

Assuming you buy any one of the listed DSLRs and a Tamron travel lens, your cost should not exceed $250 or thereabouts. You still will need a UV filter for the lens — lens caps are for amateurs — and a few other things, but that price beats by far anything new.

With one of these DSLRs in hand, no excuses: KEEP SHOOTING.

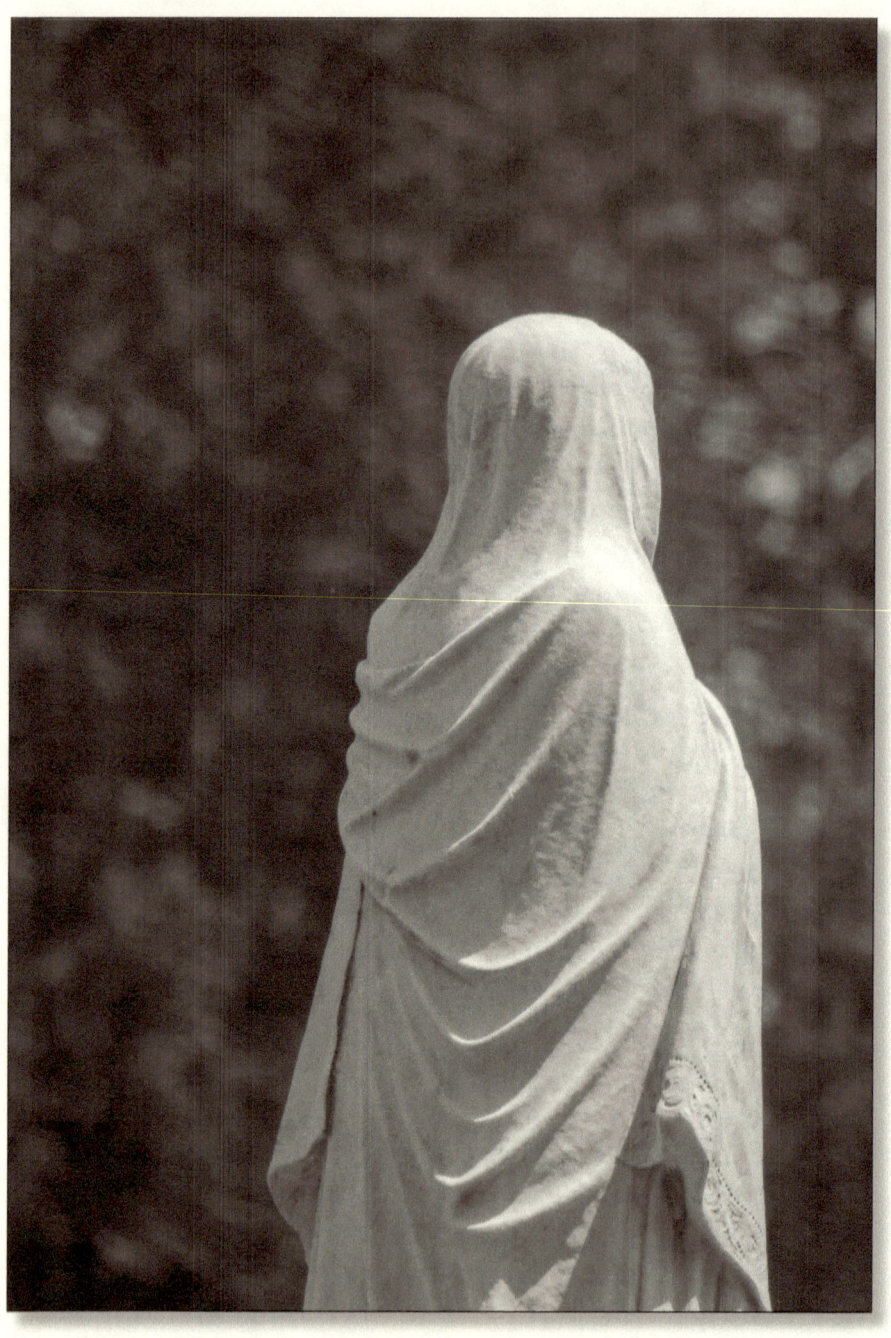

Martyrs Shrine, Auriesville, N.Y., June 17, 2015.
Nikon D7000, 300mm, 1/1250, f/5.6, ISO 200, Tv, Pattern Metering
Photo © 2015 by Shawn M. Tomlinson

Don't Worry About Your Equipment

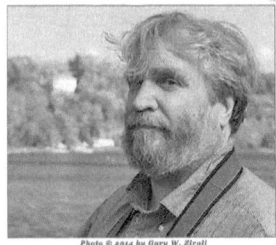

Photo © 2014 by Gary W. Ziroli

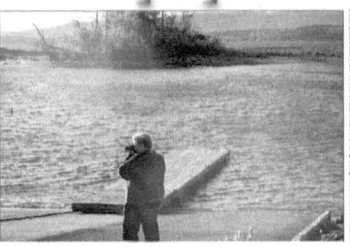

All of that said, don't worry about your equipment. Whatever DSLR you buy will give you great images. Really old ones, like Canon's D30 (not 30D) with its 3 megapixels and the Nikon D1 with its 2.65 megapixels may not give you all the detail you would like, but you still will get usable, brilliant images from them.

The point is, don't worry about how high the resolution is or what features the camera has. Learn the settings and shoot.

With an 18-200mm lens, virtually all of the main focal lengths are covered, and this will give you a lot of flexibility. Without changing lenses, you can go from wide-angle to super telephoto and everywhere in between.

Yes, DSLRs are meant to allow you to change lenses and you can do that later as you learn what focal lengths you like best and get better lenses.

Aside from flexibility, the 18-200mm lens also helps decrease the amount of dust and debris that gets inside your camera. Although this didn't matter as much with film SLRs, with DSLRs, it can cause some problems. Dust getting on the sensor can leave gray or black spots in your images, especially in photos with a lot of sky in them.

Once you have gotten the hang of the 18-200mm lens, it's time to start thinking about other lenses. Why?

Well, the travel lens is great and flexible as mentioned, but it doesn't generally have the sharpness and lack of flaws other lenses have. For example, this type of lens sometimes produces chromatic aberrations, particularly magenta. That means that, especially in bright sunshine, some of your subjects may have a magenta glow around them. This can be fixed in photo editing software such as Photoshop and Lightroom, but it's annoying. Some very good lenses have this problem, too, so it is not just due to the third-party manufacturers.

Don't be lazy. You can move closer or farther away to your subject to get the right composition with a prime lens. The image quality will far outweigh any slight inconvenience you experience.

As mentioned several times, the metadata attached to each photo's RAW file will give you information about the focal length you used. Take a look at this information over a period and that will give you an idea of the focal lengths you prefer. For example, when I shoot with the Nikon 18-55mm kit lens — yes, I use it and it's not bad — I tend to shoot at either end of the focal length range and not that much in the middle. Same thing with the Tamron 70-300mm.

What exactly should you look for in your second lens? My recommendation is a prime. You already have a wide range of focal lengths covered with the 18-200mm lens, so the next logical step would be to get a prime lens at versatile focal length. There are four that photographers prefer for various reasons. None of them will give you the extreme end of that 18-200mm.

The 24mm lens in the film days was about as wide as you could get before the image warped into fisheye territory. These days, 24mm — which equals 36mm in full-frame terms on 1.5x crop sensor cameras;

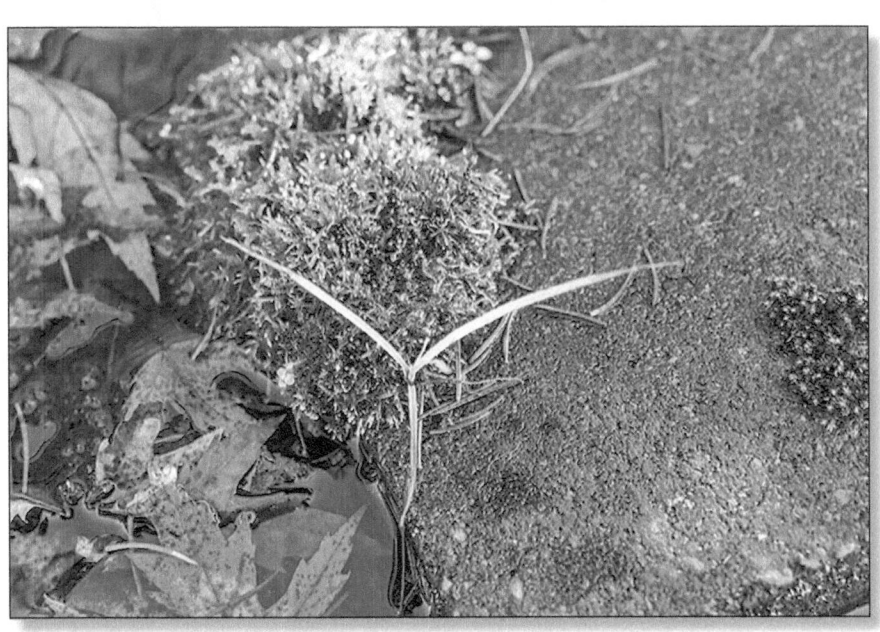

Ballston Lake, N.Y., Nov. 10, 2014.
Nikon D7000 (16.2 megapixels), 35 mm (prime), 1/125, f/5.6, ISO 400
© 2014, 2015 by Shawn M. Tomlinson

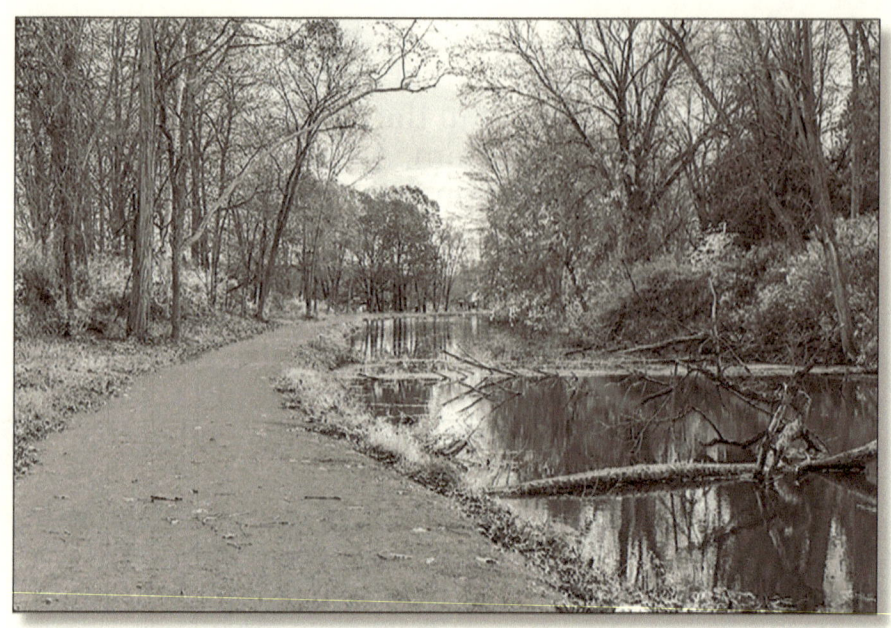

A curmudgeon and his step-granddaughter, Niskayuna, N.Y., Nov. 8, 2014.
Nikon D7000 (16.2 megapixels), 35 mm (prime), 1/500, f/5, ISO 400
© 2014, 2015 by Shawn M. Tomlinson

38.4mm on a Canon — isn't all that wide for an APS-C DSLR. Still, lens makers keep it in their lineups, largely for full-frame DSLRs. It is important to note that the main advantage of the 24mm lens is that, because it's made for full-frame cameras and thus for pros, it generally is better made than the other primes listed here.

Before the 24mm, the 28mm was the widest-angle lens that was useful. It still is. On an APS-C DSLR, it's slightly wider than a normal lens at 42mm.

Next up is the 35mm lens. This used to be the cheapest and least sought-after wide-angle lens for film SLRs, but the advent of the crop-frame sensor DSLR changed that. Instead of the poor relative of the 28mm, the 35mm now has become the prime lens many people happily use because with the crop factor, it's 52.5mm (or 56mm on Canons), which is as close to the standard film SLR lens, the 50mm, as you can get. Because of this change in use, manufacturers have put much more effort into making 35mm lenses really good, and have worked to open the aperture. Whereas a 35mm lens in the past usually had a maximum aperture of around f/2.8, today most of them are f/1.8 or, for more money, f/1.4.

The former "standard" film SLR lens, the 50mm now has become the 75mm "portrait" lens, but still is one of the more popular primes. This is helped along because Canon and Nikon make really inexpensive, mostly plastic versions with really good glass for $125 to $200.

Buying any of these primes used will save you money. The most expensive still usually is the 24mm, but not so when you get to the f/1.4 level. Even used, a 24mm f/1.4 lens can reach near $2,000. For the more reasonable f/2.8 version, it still can cost around $250. The 28mm f/2.8 usually tops out used for a little less than $175. Again, a 35mm lens at f/1.4 climbs near $2,000, but the f/1.8 version is usually less than $200.

Why, you may wonder, would you want to spend at least twice as much on the lens than on the camera body, and why on a lens with only one focal length?

The answers to the both questions are easy. Although most people think they need to spend a large amount on the camera body, they often think of the lens as the accessory. It should be the other way around. The lens has a lot more to do with image quality than the camera itself. A Velveeta (Quantaray) lens on a Nikon D4S will produce distortion, fuzziness and chromatic aberrations. A good Nikon lens, even on the lowly D3300 will produce better images than the pro DSLR with a crap lens.

The second answer is: Don't be lazy. You can move closer or farther away to your subject to get the right composition with a prime lens. The image quality will far outweigh any slight inconvenience you experience.

I can testify to this from my own recent experience.

I always used to shoot with a prime 50mm lens on my film SLR manual Pentax MX. Zoom lenses were much more expensive back then, so the prime was the way to go. Then, when autofocus came in, zooms suddenly got better and much cheaper. Instead of the 50mm lens as the standard, the new standard became, usually, a 28-80mm or 35-70mm lens.

For most of the first nine years of my work with DSLRs, I only shot with zooms because primes had gotten so much more expensive. I always knew I would buy a prime lens of some sort, but every time I

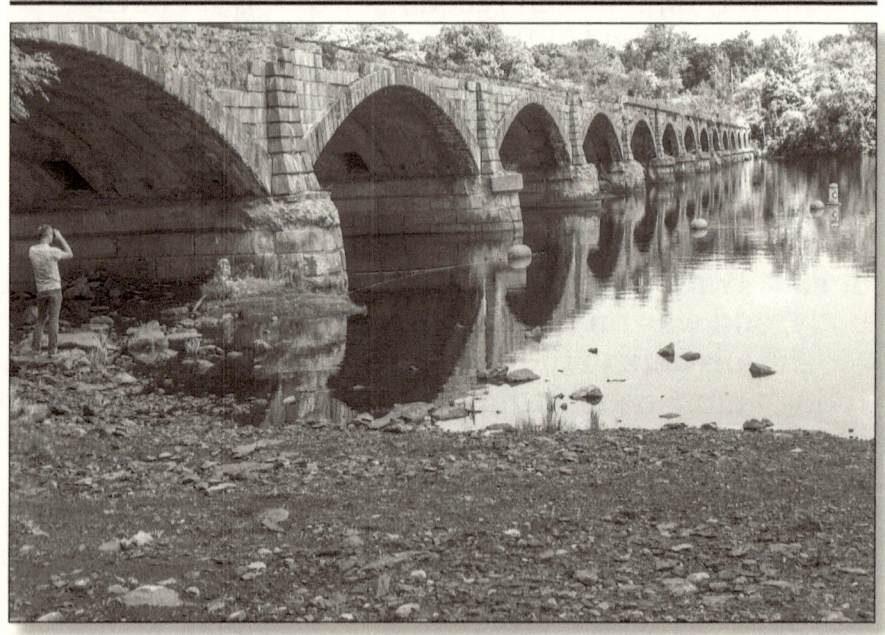

Gary Ziroli, Fort Edward, N.Y., Aug. 9, 2014.
Canon EOS 20D (8.2 megapixels), 35mm, 1/200, f/9, ISO 400
© 2014, 2015 by Shawn M. Tomlinson

got close to doing so, I opted for some zoom or other because it gave me, I believed, more flexibility.

Then, I had the opportunity to acquire a Nikon 28mm AF D f/2.8 lens. I put it on the D7000 an only twice since have used a different lens.

I grew accustom to the 28mm prime lens so quickly that I almost forget I have other lenses.

Sure, it doesn't do bokeh very well, but the sharpness is phenomenal.

Again, though, if you are just starting into this crazy world of DSLR photography, you don't need to really worry about equipment. Get a used older DSLR, an 18-200mm lens, a UV filter, an extra battery and don't look back.

For now.

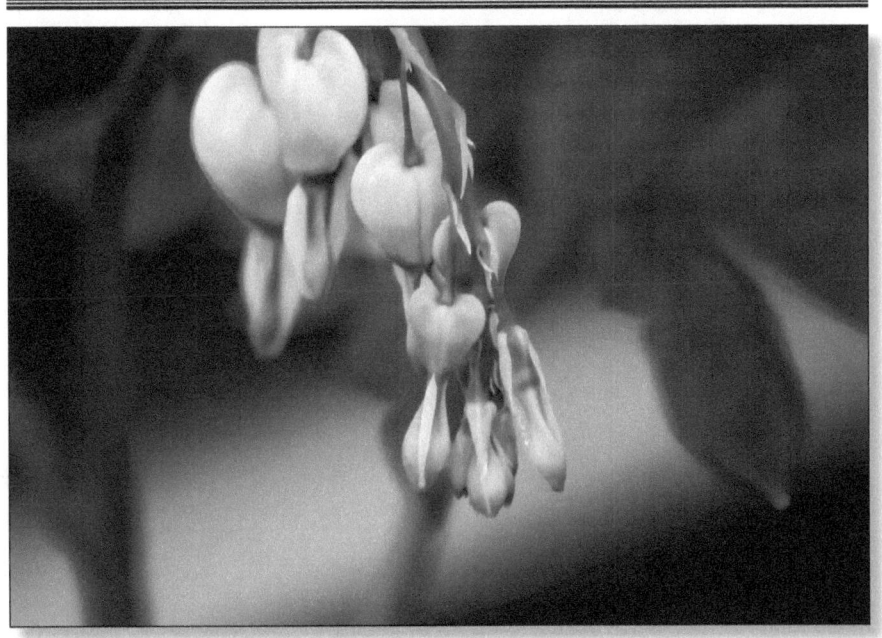

Ballston Lake, N.Y., May 18, 2015.
Nikon D2x, 300mm, 1/400, f/5.6, ISO 800, Tv, Pattern Metering
Photo © 2015 by Shawn M. Tomlinson

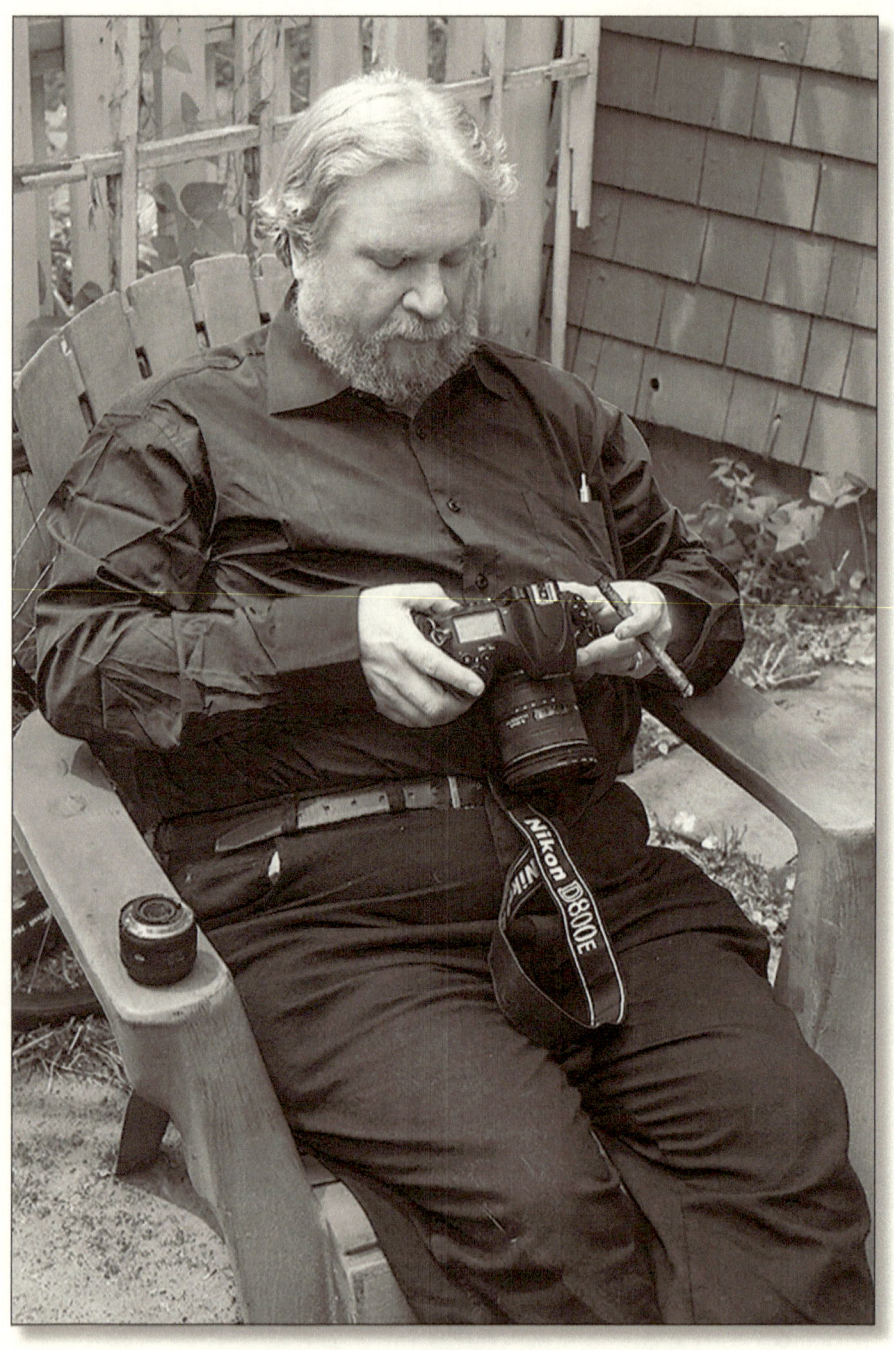

Shawn Tomlinson, Saratoga Springs, N.Y., June 27, 2015
Nikon D300 (12 megapixels), 35mm, 1/160, f/6.3, ISO 200, P, pattern metering.
© 2015 by Gary W. Ziroli

Worry About Your Equipment

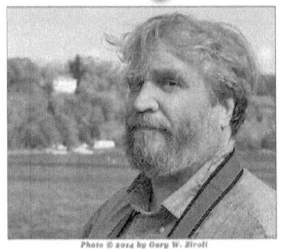

Photo © 2014 by Gary W. Ziroli

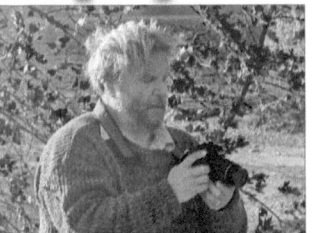

There's nothing to worry about when it comes to which DSLR you have, but there is a little to worry about in the care and feeding of the beast.

Not worry so much as concern.

Even with a pro DSLR, which is built to take a professional photographer's daily beating, every camera still needs some care.

First up is that none of the DSLRs on the the recommended list are weather sealed. That's usually reserved only for the pro models because it's expensive. Pentax, however, does weather seal its DSLRs now, but didn't yet with the *ist DS.

These cameras will take some rain and snow, but it's not a good idea to keep them out in bad conditions for too long. They also don't handle really cold conditions well and will stop working at some lower temperatures, so keeping one of them in your trunk in the winter should be avoided.

Then there's this UV filter thing I keep mentioning. There's some debate amongst photographers about using UV filters, but I do not really participate in it. As far as I'm concerned, UV filters are absolute necessities for all lenses.

The reason is that a UV filter protect the front element of the lens. Even the best UV filters — which are essential; you don't want bad glass in a filter in front of good glass in a lens — are far less expensive to replace than lenses. UV filters are easier to clean than lenses, as well.

I never use lens caps. Most pros don't. They get in the way and are easily lost. And I know this is obvious, but they only protect lenses when they are attached to them and you can't take photographs that way.

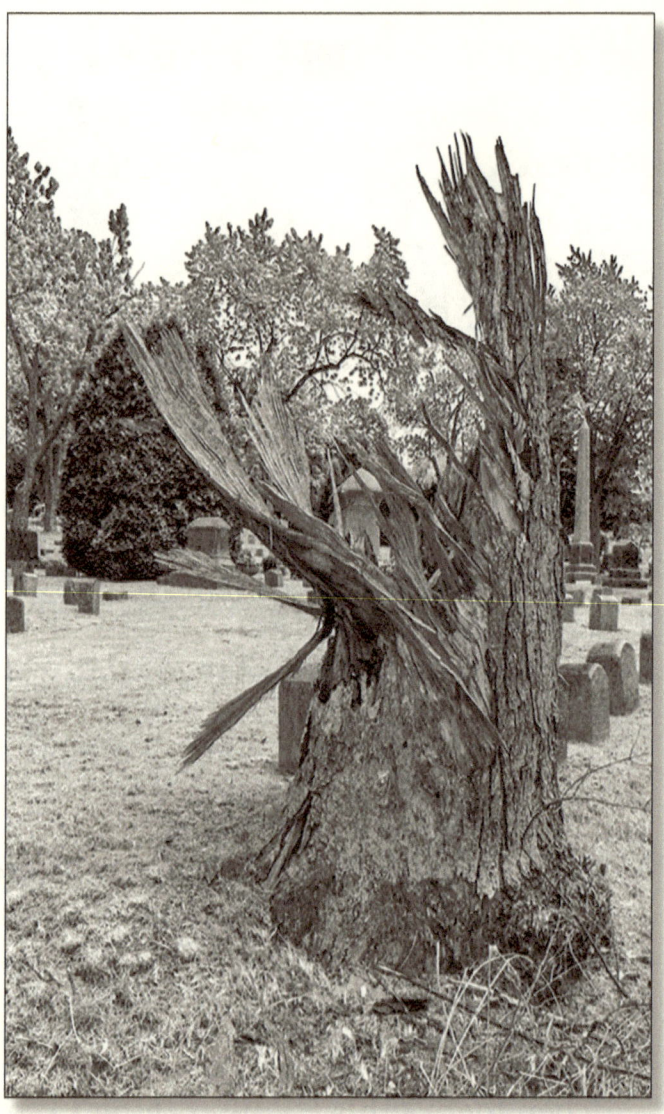

Johnstown, N.Y., June 29, 2005.
Pentax *ist DS (6.1 megapixels), 18 mm, 1/180, f/22, ISO 1600
© 2014, 2015 by Shawn M. Tomlinson

Spending the little extra money to protect the lens will prove very cost-effective, especially noticeable the first time you inadvertently hit the lens on something.

The number on the front of the lens that isn't focal length tells you what size UV filter you need. The most common sizes are 52mm, 58mm, 62mm and 77mm. Manufacturers who make the best UV filters include Tiffen, Hoya and Canon.

Don't waste money on a no-name brand filter on eBay. It's just as bad as putting a Velveeta (Quantaray) lens on a good DSLR and expecting clear images.

And now to the most difficult part of taking care of your equipment, the part that keeps photographers awake at night.

Cleaning the sensor.

The camera manufacturers recommend strongly against doing this yourself. Partially that's so they make the money in cleaning them, but mostly it's because doing it yourself can destroy your DSLR if you

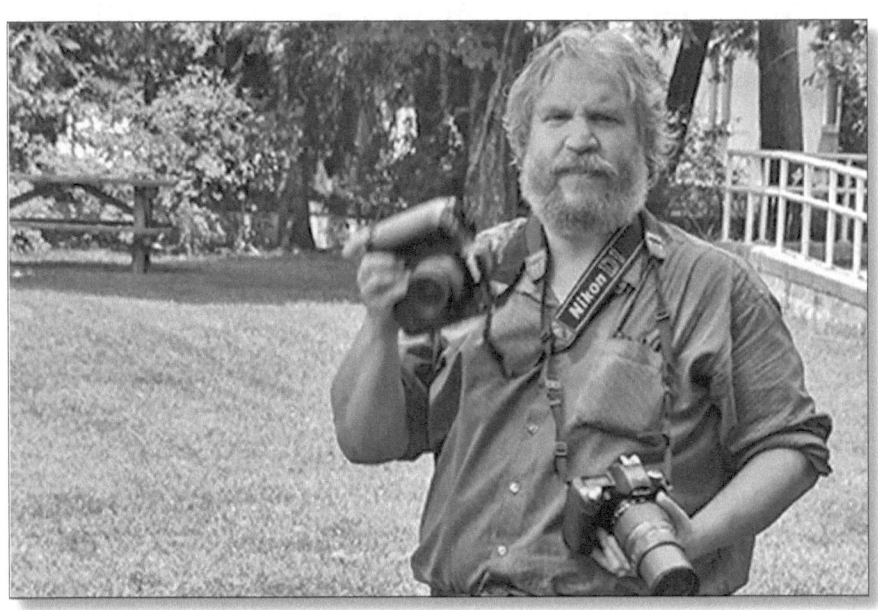

Shawn M. Tomlinson as shot by Gary W. Ziroli, Lincoln Baths, Saratoga Springs, N.Y., Aug. 5, 2014.
Pentax K10D (10.2 megapixels), 53 mm, 1/90, f/5.6, ISO 100
© 2014, 2015 by Gary W. Ziroli

are not VERY careful.

The problem is dust gets into the chamber behind the lens essentially every time you change lenses. When it settles on the sensor, it causes gray or black spots in your images.

The safest way to "fix" it is to not fix it, but to clone out the spots in Photoshop. If you shoot a lot — and you should be — this can get really tedious. It generally works, though, so if you do not feel safe cleaning your camera, stick with this.

However, consider that you are paying not a lot of money for any of these DSLRs and if you did happen to damage your camera, it would not take much to replace it. That's another advantage of buying older DSLRs.

And honestly, if you are careful, you can clean the sensor routinely and not have any problems.

I was scared to do it the first time, but repeated necessity has made me much more at ease. I'm still very careful.

You're not really cleaning the sensor itself. Although anti-aliasing are being eliminated now in new cameras, they were built in most of them for years. Such a filter is a thin piece of glass or plastic over the sensor. It works to decrease moire, which is an effect that occurs sometimes when you photograph lined surfaces.

So, you actually are cleaning this filter, not the sensor.

The first thing to try because it does not involve touching the sensor and filter is some form of blower. I've heard some daring souls have used dry vacs to suck out all the debris, but this worries me because it could take the mirror and sensor with it, however unlikely.

Safer is something like an ear cleaning syringe, although those do not really have the power you may need. Most pros who acknowledge you may clean your own sensor recommend the Giottos Rocket Air Blaster. It's less than $10 and worth a try.

Blowing air into your DSLR body works best if you hold the camera with the lens mount down. Gravity then can take loosened dust particles away.

If this no-touch method doesn't work — and it often doesn't — you need something a little more direct.

What it takes is a sensor cleaning kit. These range from relatively inexpensive to quite expensive. The kit I use is closer to the lower end of the range. It has plastic wands with cleaning material attached to each one. I add a drop of cleaner to the wand, and make one firm but gentle pass in each direction.

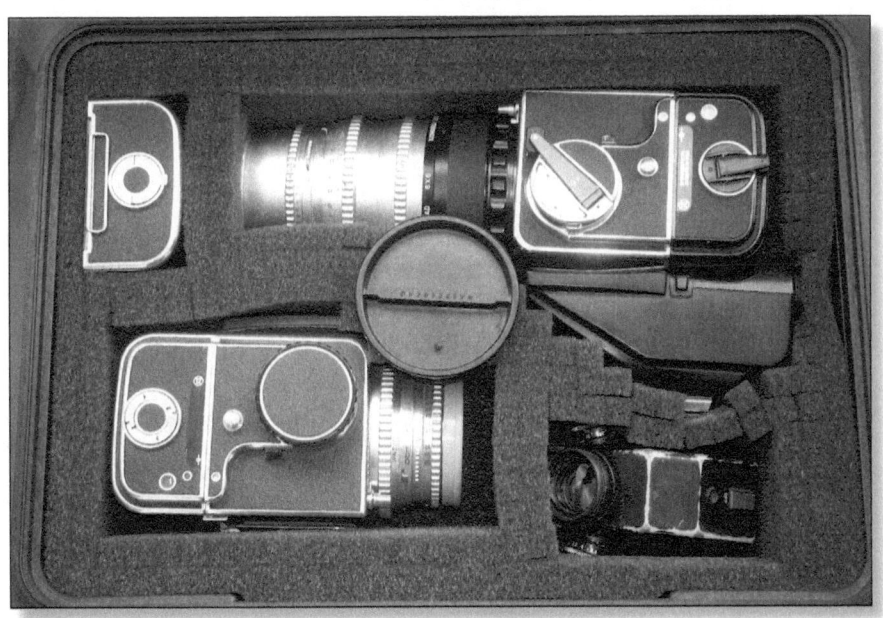

The Hasselblads sit securely in a Pelican water-tight case, Ballston Lake, N.Y., Aug. 11, 2008.
Pentax *ist DS (6.1 megapixels), 40mm, 1/90, f/5.6, ISO 3200
© 2008, 2015 by Shawn M. Tomlinson

It may take several cleanings to get the sensor where you want it.

After you clean it, reattach the lens, go outside and shoot some images with bright blue sky.

Then look at the images in Photoshop to see how effective your cleaning was. It can be frustrating because sometimes, you just move the dust particles around. Sometimes, it gets worse.

This is why I said you may need to clean it several times before you get it as spotless as possible.

It is true that most recent DSLRs have built-in sensor-cleaning systems, but they don't always work perfectly, either, so it is common to need those cleaned as well.

It's just a lot less scary on a $100 DSLR than on a $1,000 camera.

One last thing, which also may be obvious. Keep your DSLR and lenses in your gadget bag whenever you aren't using them. A good gadget bag offers both portability and some protection for your gear.

Some people use hard-shelled cases such as those made by Zero Halliburton and Pelican, and these are great and safe cases. I use a Pelican for my Hasselblad. The problem is these are quite expensive — Zero Halliburtons start at around $325 — and they are cumbersome and not handy.

I prefer Tamrac, but there are other good gadget bag makers out there. I use two Tamrac bags. The first is a small one for just a DSLR body, lens, battery and flash. My main bag is a Pro 8 that holds two DSLR bodies, lenses, a flash, filters, multiple memory cards, cleaning kit, charger and virtually everything I need for a Voyage of Photography.

I don't, however, carry it around when I shoot. It's big and heavy and gets in the way. Instead, it is the place I keep all the equipment at home and take in the car. When I get out to shoot, I take the camera — or sometimes two — around my neck and leave the Tamrac in the car. I've seen too many people struggle with gadget bags — even pros — during a shoot, and the few times I've had to carry the bag with me, it has drastically cut my shooting.

And that never is a good thing.

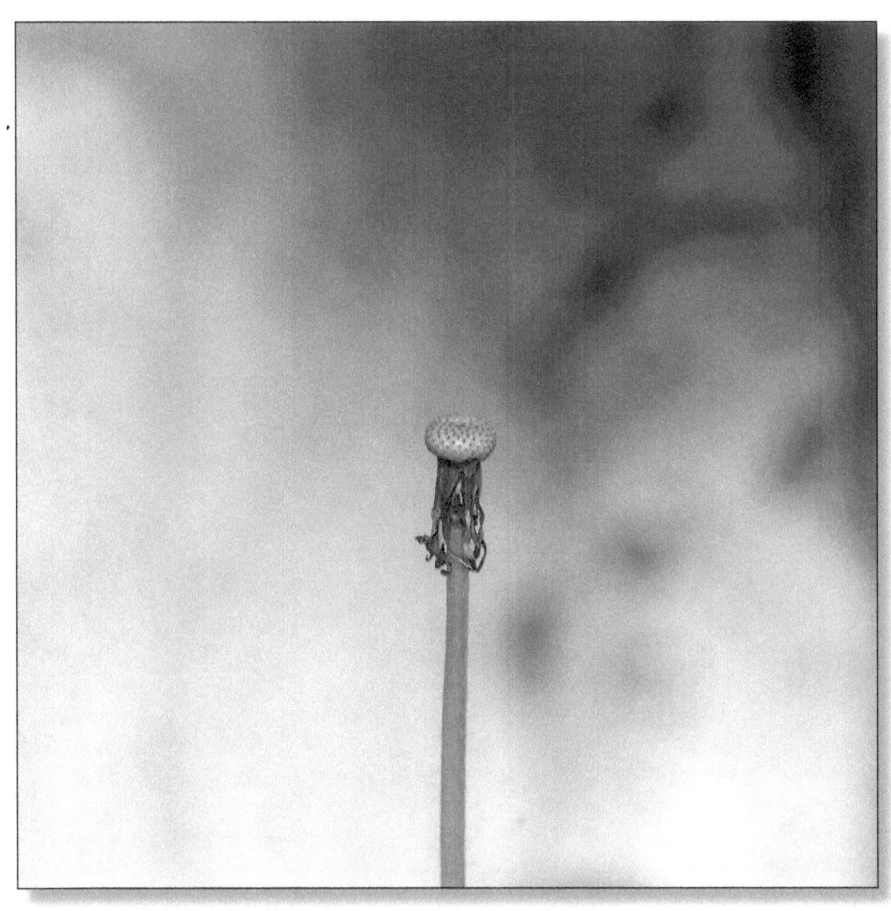

Ballston Lake, N.Y., May 22, 2015.
Nikon D2x, 300mm, 1/640, f/11, ISO 400, Tv, Pattern Metering
Photo © 2015 by Shawn M. Tomlinson

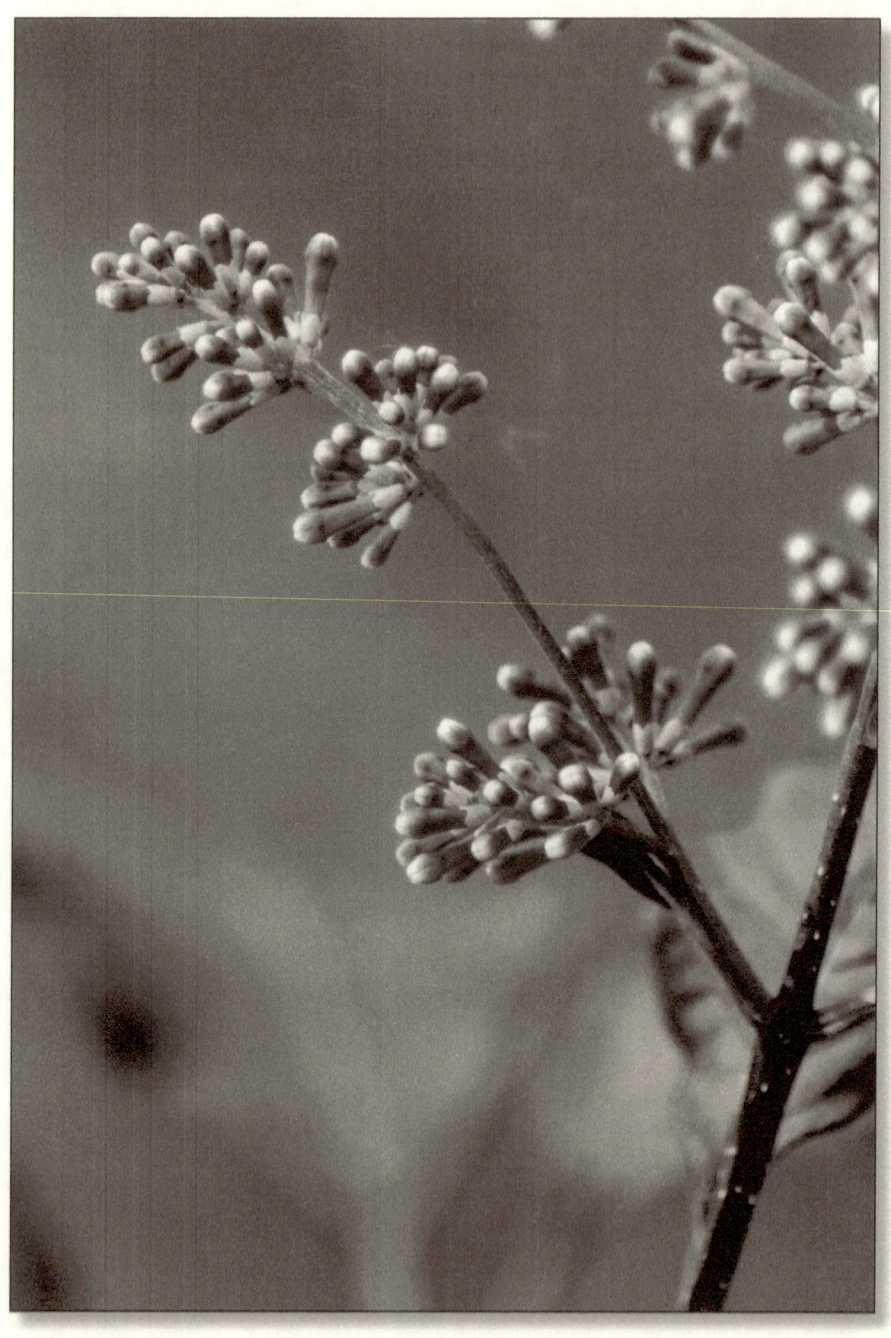

Ballston Lake, N.Y., May 30, 2015.
Nikon D2x, 300mm, 1/500, f/5.6, ISO 640, Tv, Pattern Metering
Photo © 2015 by Shawn M. Tomlinson

Go to Pretty Places

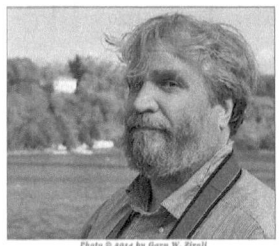

The 12 Steps of Photography

Step 8

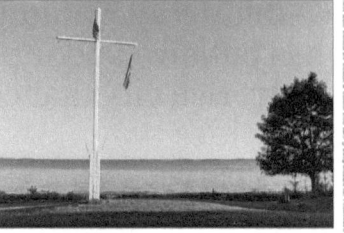

Photo © 2014 by Gary W. Ziroll

It's fantastic to set aside money and use it to go to exotic locations to practice your photography, to get those unbelievable shots that come along once in a lifetime. I highly recommend it.

Since you most likely won't be able to do this every day — and you need to shoot every day — it is useful to become familiar with interesting and pretty places within a certain distance from home. Pick a distance from your place and look at detailed maps and Google Earth to see all the interesting locations. There will be some.

For all-day photo voyages, I go farther afield, maybe up to 50 miles from home. For the other days, when I have less time, I usually stay within 10 miles, often five or fewer.

I know this sounds dull at first, but consider this. There is virtually no place you could take me where I would fail to find interesting photographic subjects and shoot at least 100 images.

No place.

As an example, I usually go out on Voyages of Photography with Gary Ziroli once or twice a week. We go to other locations, but many times, we just walk around Saratoga Springs. We walk different streets, but essentially it is the same place week to week. I rarely come away from each of these walking tours with fewer than 300 images. Not all are exhibition quality, but some are.

Admittedly, Saratoga Springs — which seems like it has outlawed poor people; and it's just the sort of snooty, rich city that could do that — is one of the safest cities in this part of the world. I never have fear walking its streets, fear of bodily harm or, worse, fear of camera theft. It could happen, I suppose, but in general, the advantage of its population having so much money is that they can afford significant police presence, which keeps the crime rate low.

Back in the 1960s and 1970s,

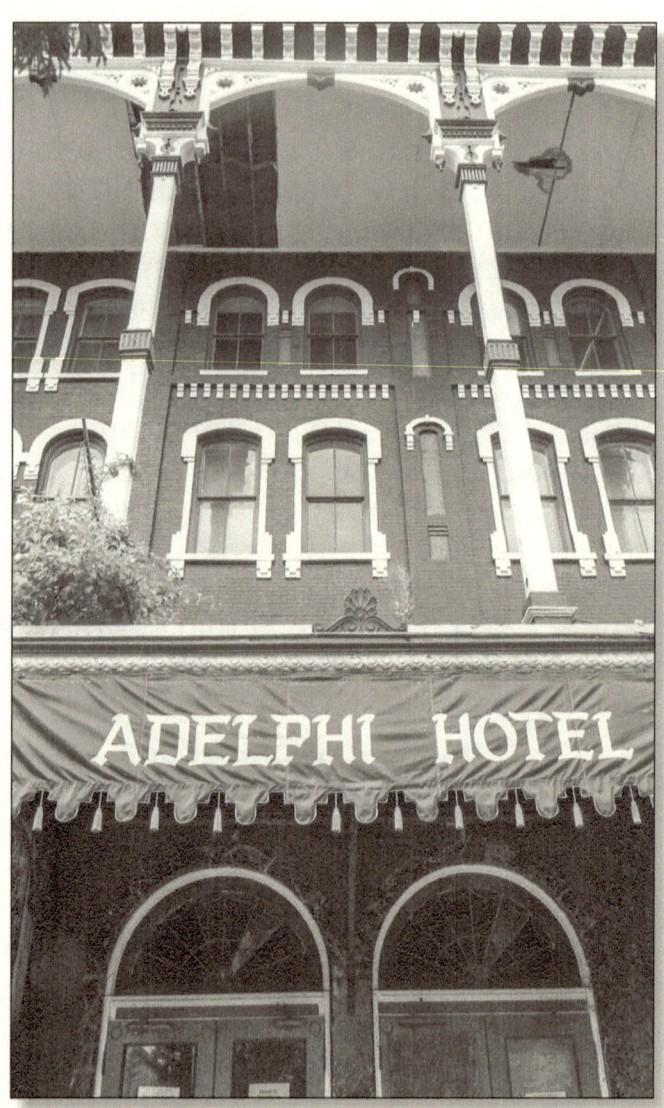

Empty Adelphi Hotel, Saratoga Springs, N.Y., Aug. 23, 2014.
Nikon D1X 5.47 megapixels), 18mm, 1/200, f/11, ISO 400
© 2014, 2015 by Shawn M. Tomlinson

Saratoga Springs was a dump. Except for the August thoroughbred racing season, it was a poor, dirty, nasty little city. Then a concerted effort brought it back and made it cleaner and more sparkling than ever. The result is the above mentioned safety, but the other result is that older, more interesting buildings and neighbor-

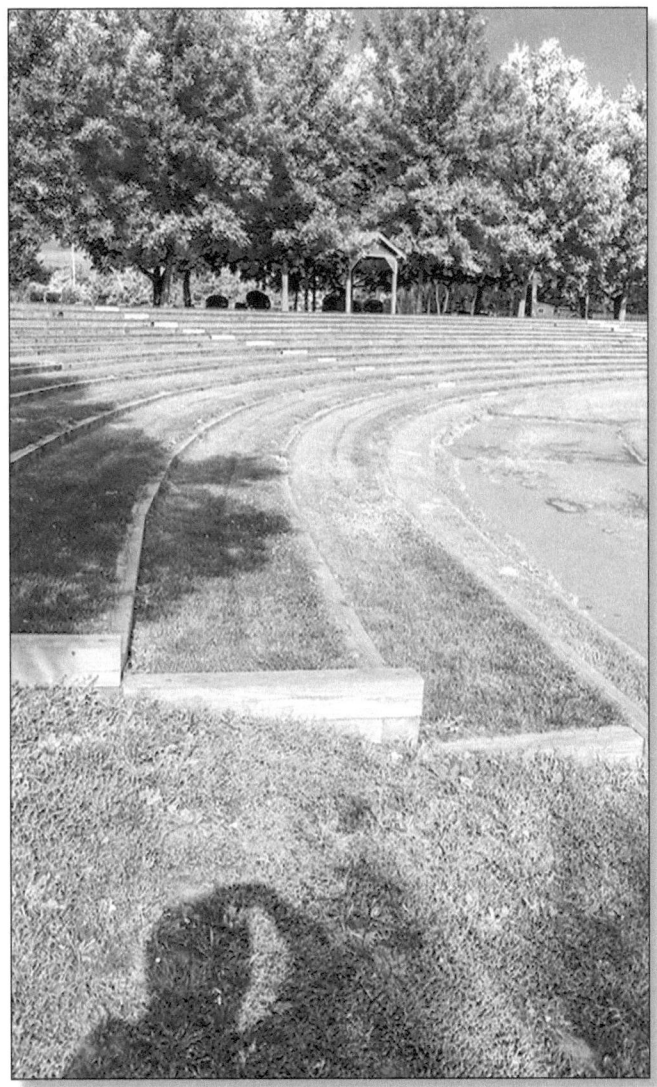

Shawn M. Tomlinson, Scotia, N.Y., Oct. 2, 2014.
Nikon D7000 (16.2 megapixels), 18 mm, 1/1000, f/6.3, ISO 250
© 2014, 2015 by Shawn M. Tomlinson

hoods fall victim routinely to the onslaught of yuppie condos and elite boutiques.

Saratoga Springs once boasted the grandest, largest, most ornate hotel in the world. It was called the Grand Union Hotel. When the city began to hit the

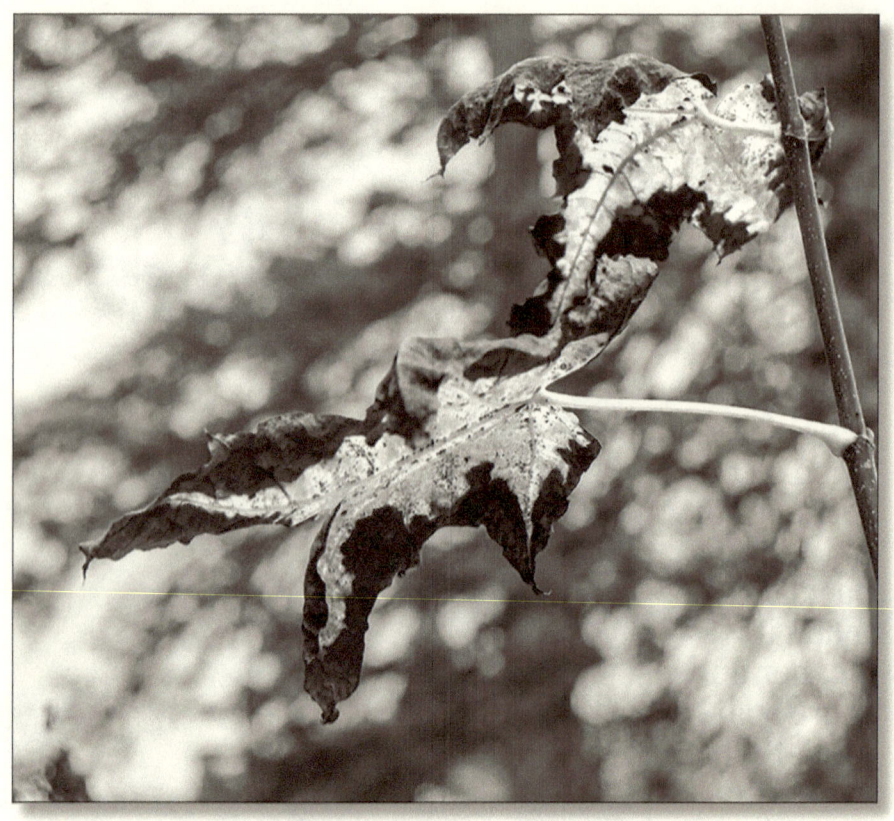

Saratoga Springs, N.Y., Oct. 28, 2014.
Nikon D7000 (16.2 megapixels), 55 mm, 1/320, f/6.3, ISO 250
© 2014, 2015 by Shawn M. Tomlinson

skids in the 1950s, the wreckers took the 100-plus-year-old structure and left in its wake, ironically, a Grand Union supermarket. That too has disappeared.

In the place where the Grand Union Hotel once covered an entire block with 1,000 guest rooms, several ornate dining rooms and its own opera house, now stands vitally essential things such as a Baby Gap store.

So, part of the reason Gary and I — both historians in our own ways — like to photograph Saratoga Springs is that many of the best buildings we shoot today may be gone literally tomorrow.

We do not restrict ourselves to this city. We like other relatively nearby municipalities, too, and we have discovered a love for the locks on the Champlain Canal that line the Hudson River. Various lakes, rivers and parks around the area also provide many photographic opportunities, often in unexpected ways.

For example, Gary and I returned to Greenwich this summer because we had glimpsed an interesting dam on the Batten Kill River on our previous visit, but could not find a way to get to it and didn't have time to look very long. This time, we found a good place to get an overview of the dam and river, and discovered something unexpected along the way.

We parked two streets over and as we walked toward the river cliff, we came across a small, triangular

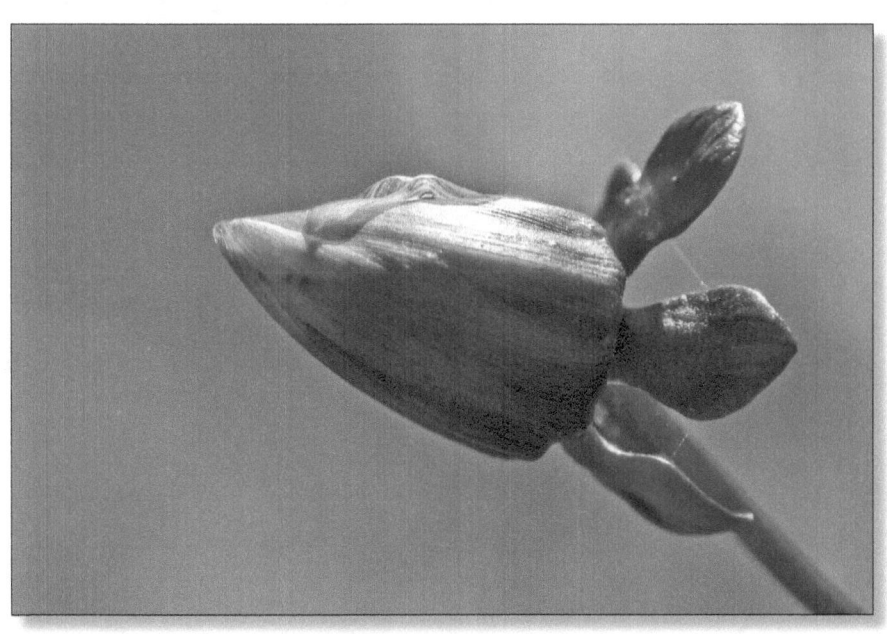

Greenwich, N.Y., Aug. 30, 2014.
Nikon D70 (6.1 megapixels), 270mm, 1/1600, f/5.6, ISO 400
© 2014, 2015 by Shawn M. Tomlinson

park. It had such great flowers on such a bright, sunny day, we stopped to photograph it. I produced a small photo eBook of it titled The Three-Sided Park. The park was not the destination because we didn't know it was there. Yet it proved to be quite photogenic.

My wife, Carole, and I also make some Voyages of Photography, though not as many as we would like. Her favorite spot is a small boat launch we both drove by for years without noticing. The Union College Crew Team practices on the Mohawk River there near Freeman's Bridge. The old, abandoned supports for a previous bridge still stand, and there is an old iron railroad bridge just north of the boat launch, and many ducks gather there — Carole's favorite part — so there is plenty to photograph.

Likewise, I wanted to walk across the bridge over the Mohawk that serves as access to the Thruway near Rotterdam Junction. I found that the only way to do it

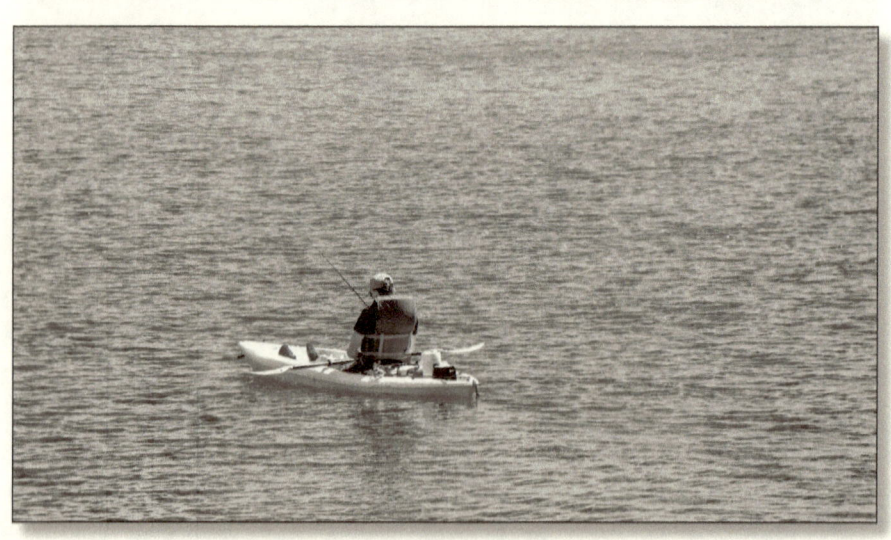

Kiwanis Park, Mohawk River, Rotterdam Junction, N.Y., July 20, 2014.
Pentax K20D (14.2 megapixels) 200mm, 1/500, f/8, ISO 200
© 2014, 2015 by Shawn M. Tomlinson

was to park at a park-and-ride lot and follow the bike trail I never knew was there. This led to following the train quite a distance and discovering where it went and what was there. Carole and I found the Rotterdam Kiwanis Park there at Plotter Kill that also yielded some good photos.

You can just wander or drive around to find interesting locations. I do. But a combination of this and looking at maps will get you to some places you never knew were there.

Sure, save the money and go to the Taj Mahal and Machu Picchu and Yosemite and every place else you want to go. Shoot as many images as you can.

Just don't disregard the region you live in. You will find many, many interesting photographic subjects, all within a few minutes walk or drive.

Don't believe me? Bring me there and I'll guide you.

And I'll get lots of great images myself.

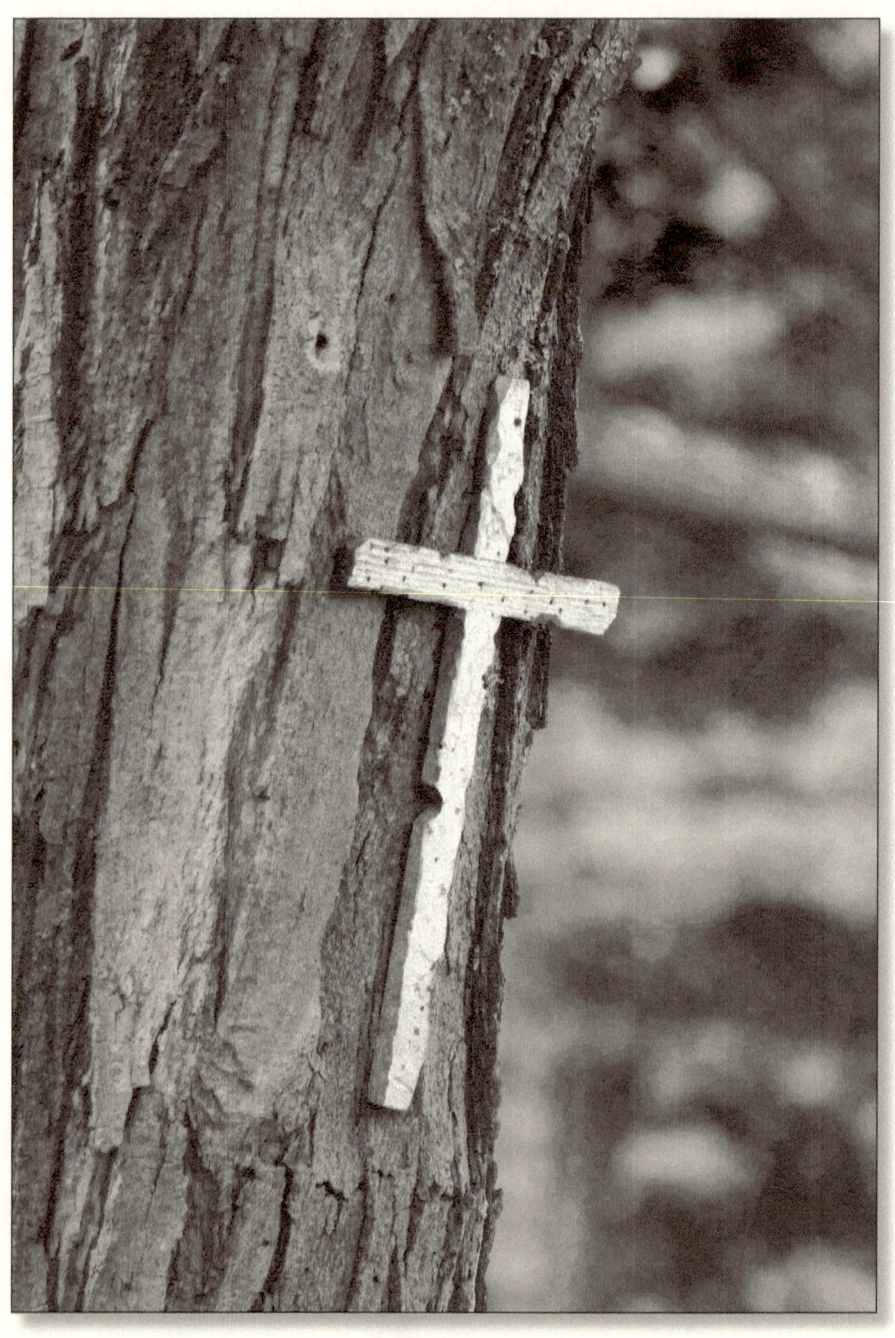

Martyrs Shrine, Auriesville, N.Y., June 17, 2015.
Nikon D7000, 270mm, 1/1250, f/5.3, ISO 200, Tv, Pattern Metering
Photo © 2015 by Shawn M. Tomlinson

Stay Home

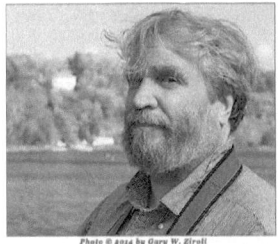

Photo © 2014 by Gary W. Ziroli

The 12 Steps of Photography

Step 9

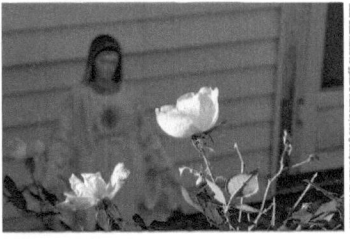

I admit it started because there are just some days when it's difficult to get away from the house because of various commitments, tasks, laziness, etc.

It got more important when I broke my second foot and found it very difficult to maneuver too much.

Yet, after these things got better, I still stay home to shoot often.

I live in a typical suburban home with a small front yard, a fenced-in backyard and a wetland behind that. My wife, Carole, long before she knew me had many flowers and other plants installed on the small property, and she likes things like birdbaths, old milk containers, etc., so they were there, too.

Some of these things are gone now because of landscaping and gardening — not done by me — to clean out the weeds and overgrowth that sprang up because Carole no longer has time to work on it and, let's face it, I haven't a clue about how to make the right things grow and the wrong things go away.

I realize not everyone lives on this type of property, but that doesn't really matter. Learn to extrapolate.

I don't shoot at home every day, but when I do, the big bouncy rottwieller named Baby is eager for us to shoot together in her fenced area in the back. She even occasionally has pawed my Tamrac gadget bag where she knows the cameras reside to let me know it's time to go out and shoot.

Some-times, she gets me to do this even when I'm not plan-ning on it. Just today, my plan was to fi-nally shoot some things inside the house I had been eying for some time. I did that for a while, and then Baby was there with her panting

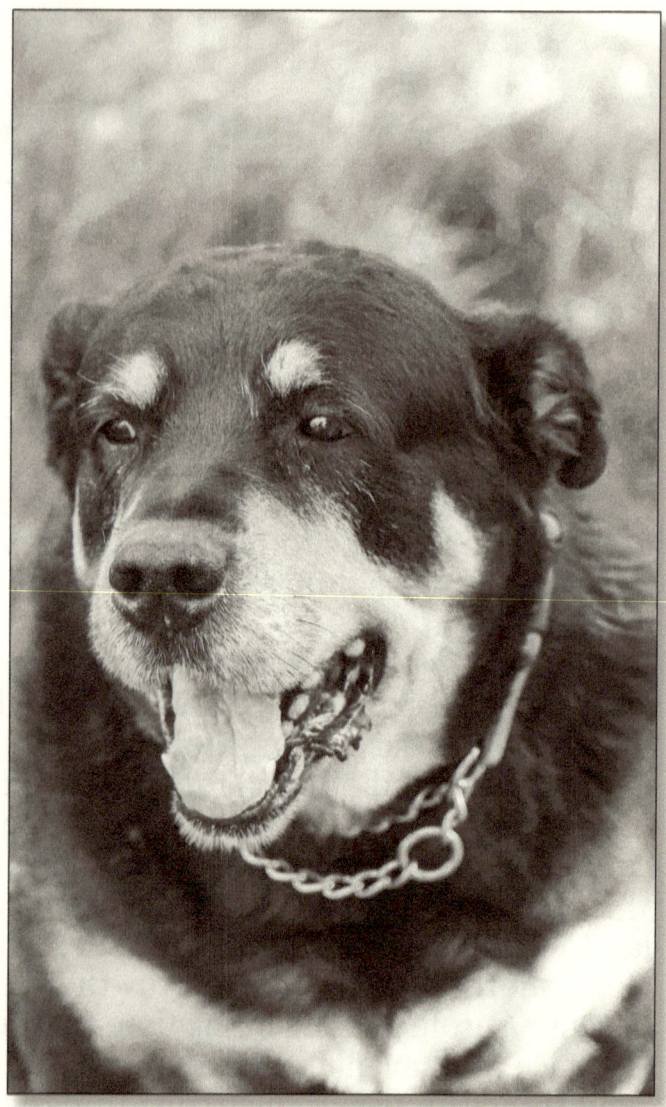

Baby, Ballston Lake, N.Y., Nov. 2, 2014.
Nikon D7000 (16.2 megapixels), 70mm, 1/1000, f/4, ISO 400
© 2014, 2015 by Shawn M. Tomlinson

smile doing the "Baby Dance" and eying the Nikon D7000 in my hands. She needed to go out anyway, so I let us both out in the backyard. She immediately ate some snow — something she loves almost as much as

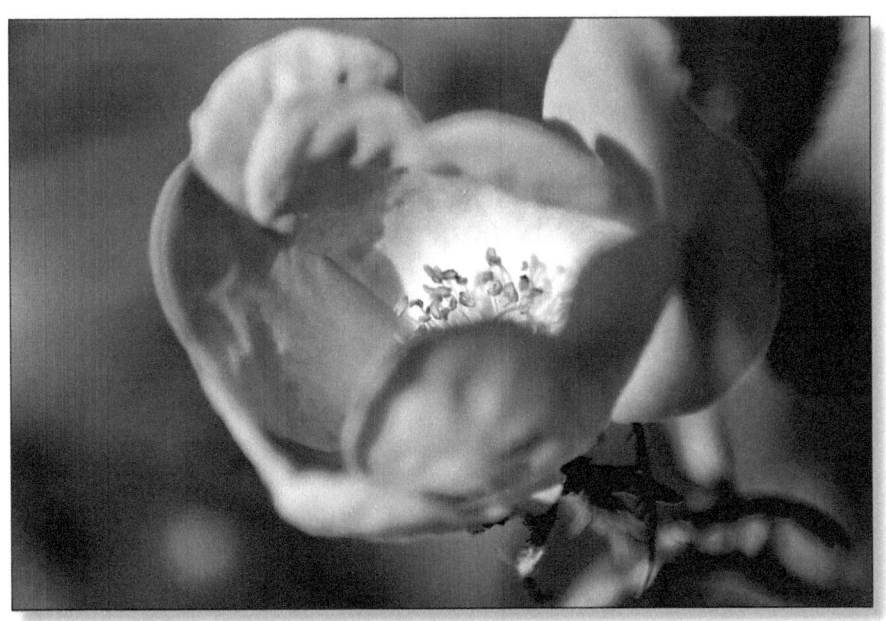

Ballston Lake, N.Y., Nov. 2, 2014.
Nikon D7000 (16.2 megapixels), 300mm, 1/1000, f/7.1, ISO 400
© 2014, 2015 by Shawn M. Tomlinson

having her picture taken — and we headed down the steps from the deck.

It was a very gray day, but it was warmer than it had been, so the two of us wandered around the yard. I was shooting her and other things — dead leaves till poignantly on branches, the wetland beyond the fence, the empty pool, the yellow plastic pig, Baby's newest toy — and she was frolicking, rolling around on her back, another of her favorite things.

After a while, well, the mail should have been in the box by then, so I went alone to the front yard — there is no fence and Baby doesn't like the psychotic convicted felon across the street — photographing interesting things — ice in a plastic garbage pale lid, the faded whirly pig my wife placed in the one-time garden, the deep green and wet moss on the old dying tree — on the way to the mailbox.

The flowers are all gone in early December, but there still are interesting things there. I have photographed some of them many times, under many lighting conditions. Others are new or appear new to me.

I shot 76 images indoors and 75 more outdoors. A low shooting day for me, but there are some good photos in there.

When I go to my friend and photographic colleague, Gary Ziroli's home in Saratoga Springs, we often do the same things. He lives on a service alley and has a small courtyard. We often sit there to talk and smoke, and we almost always have our cameras with us. Gary usually shoots with a Nikon D300 these days, but occasionally with his Nikon D1X. I almost always have the D7000 in my hands, but sometimes have

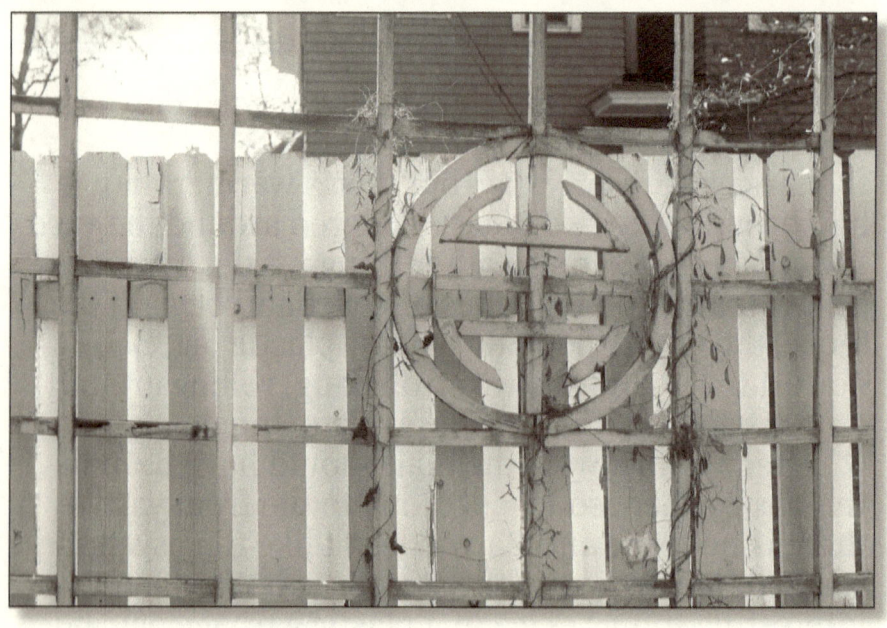

Gary's Courtyard, Saratoga Springs, N.Y., Nov. 8, 2014.
Nikon D7000 (16.2 megapixels), 35mm (prime), 1/1000, f/5, ISO 400
© 2014, 2015 by Shawn M. Tomlinson

the Nikon D70 or D1, or the Canon EOS 20D. Rarely these days, I have the Pentax K20D around my neck.

As we sit there smoking, we look around the same scene we've seen countless times. The multitude of squirrels that live in the area play around bouncing from branch to branch, occasionally venturing into the

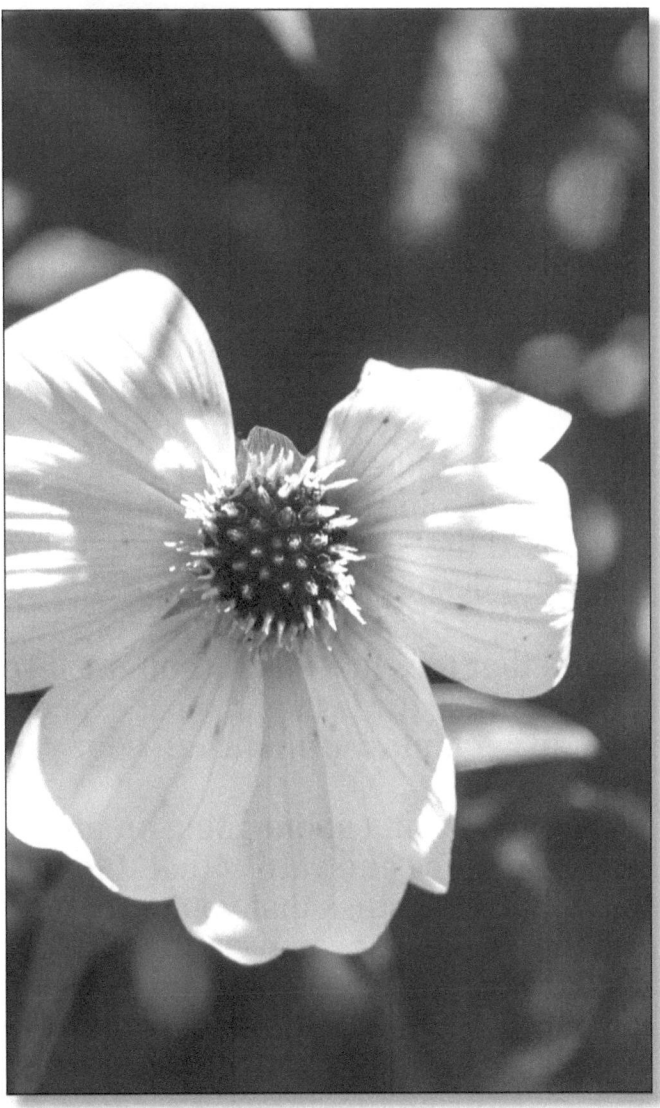

Greenwich, N.Y., Aug. 30, 2014.
Nikon D70 (6.1 megapixels), 300mm, 1/1600, f/6, ISO 400
© 2014, 2015 by Shawn M. Tomlinson

courtyard to stare at us. Birds, particularly Blue Jays and Cardinals, for some reason, fly in and out.

Because the road is/was a service alley, it doesn't get a lot of traffic. It does get some very interesting light at different times of the day and year. We often shoot that courtyard. When we are testing out new lenses or cameras, or exposures or ISO settings, we also often photograph each other, so there are many photos of Gary and of me sitting or standing there.

The point is that, no matter where you live, you have abundant photographic possibilities right there without going any place else.

Just this evening I was going through some photos from early November — I've been writing a lot these days, so I am way behind on photo processing, even though I continue to shoot every day — and was astonished at some of the color and some of the shots. I had used the $29 Tamron LD 70-300mm lens for them and despite it not being the sharpest or best in the world, it does capture some amazing images.

And that tells me — and should tell you — that it doesn't take the best and most expensive equipment to get fantastic photos. In your yard and in your home.

The great thing about going on photo shoots in your own home and yard is that it forces you to learn to really "See" things that you never noticed before and that makes for some great images. It also trains you how to look for — and what to look for — interesting photographic subjects no matter where you are.

I plan a series of photo eBooks just of my house and yard during the different seasons. These eBooks will contain some of my best work, and I didn't have to go to Big Sur or the Reichenbach Falls to get them. Although, I wish I had taken a camera when I was at Big Sur and driving up and down the Pacific Coast Highway. I didn't. Oh well.

You probably will think the whole stay at home to photograph things idea is stupid or dull before you do it. It isn't. Consider it a lesson along the way to the greatness that your photography will be. Look at everything. See the light and how it works on the mailbox or the front door knob or the flowers or the scattered leaves on the walk. Pay attention to tiny details.

And shoot.

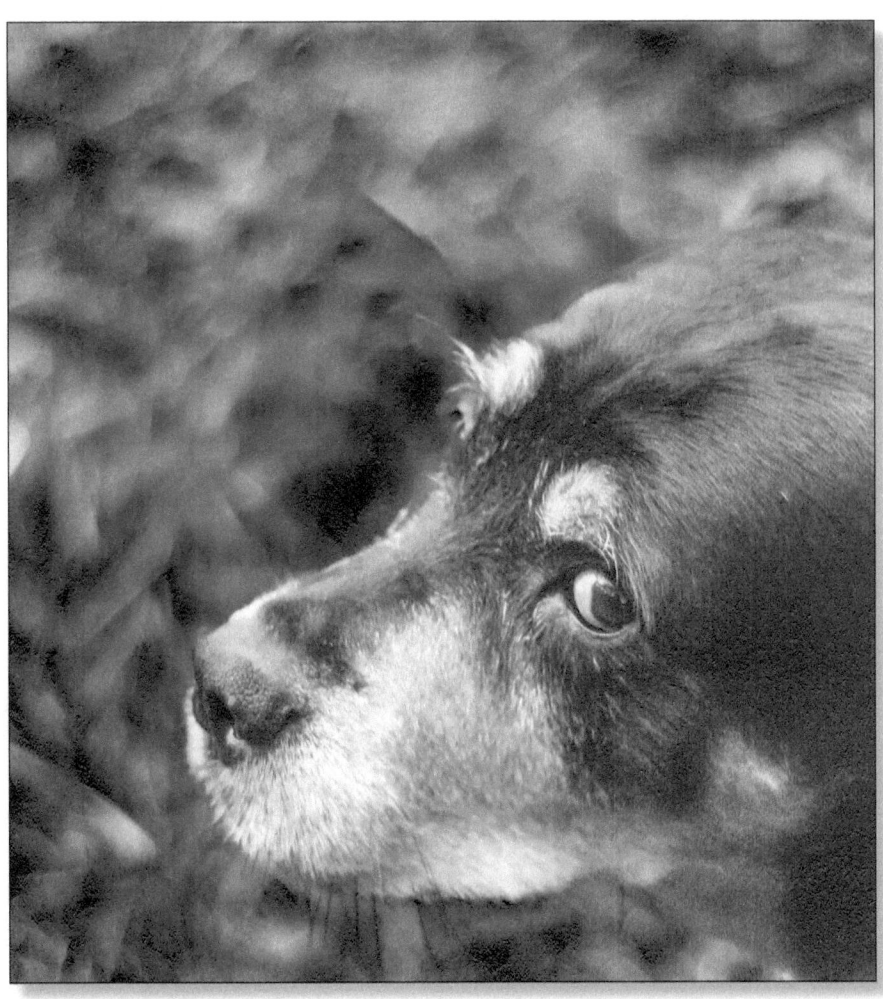

Baby, Ballston Lake, N.Y., June 1, 2015.
Nikon D2x, 50mm, 1/1000, f/1.8, ISO 1600, Tv, Pattern Metering
Photo © 2015 by Shawn M. Tomlinson

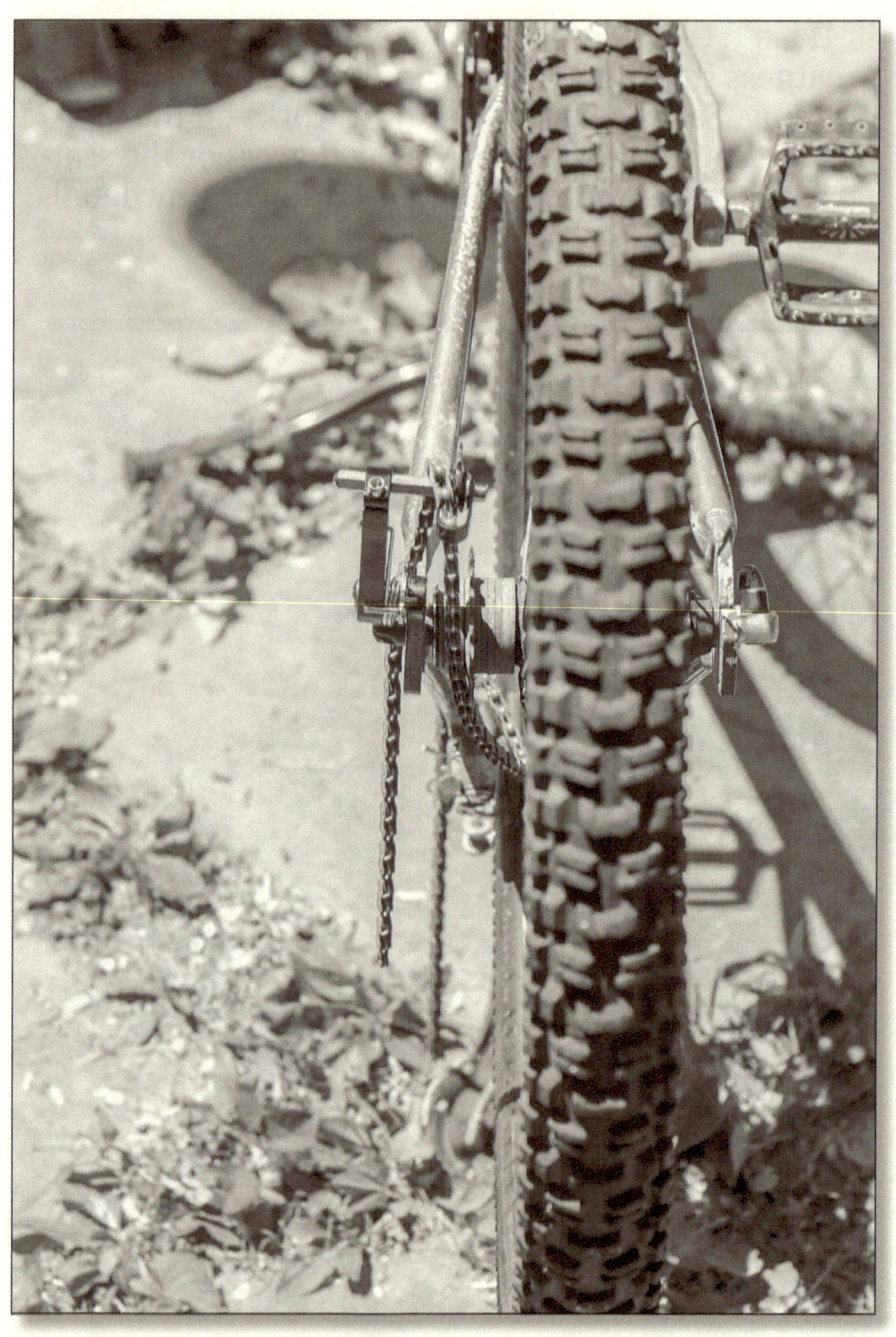

Saratoga Springs, N.Y., May 23, 2015.
Nikon D7000, 50mm, 1/1000, f/5, ISO 200, Tv, Pattern Metering
Photo © 2015 by Shawn M. Tomlinson

Don't Rely Upon Post-Processing

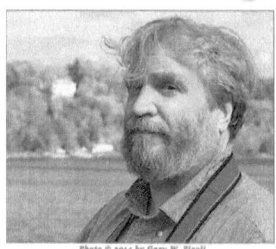

Photo © 2014 by Gary W. Biroli

The 12 Steps of Photography
Step 10

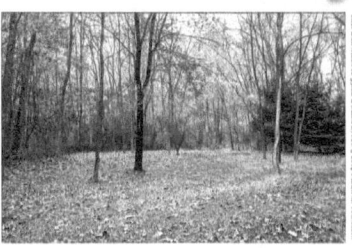

I loved working in the darkroom.

Even the smells of the deadly photographic chemicals made me happy. And now make me nostalgic for the "good ol' days" of film.

I loved coming home with a couple of freshly shot rolls of black and white film — usually Kodak Tri-X Pan or T-Max or Ilford HP5 — setting up the film tank and reel, making sure the film leader was sticking out of the 35mm cartridge (or, when I was smart, having a bottle opener ready), turning off the lights and threading the film into the reel, hoping it was going in correctly, then sealing the film tank and turning on the light.

After a dozen rolls or so of mistakes, I could rely upon my learned skill to develop black and white film.

When it came later to placing the negatives in the enlarger and making prints... well, not so much.

I loved doing it. I just never got any good at it.

So, imagine how much I was thrilled when I got those free evaluation copies of Photoshop 1.0 and Digital Darkroom 1.0 for the Mac.

Except, of course, at the time photos weren't digital; they were on film. This meant everything had to be scanned, and as with all new technology, scanners were expensive and didn't work all that well unless you bought the top models just for scanning film.

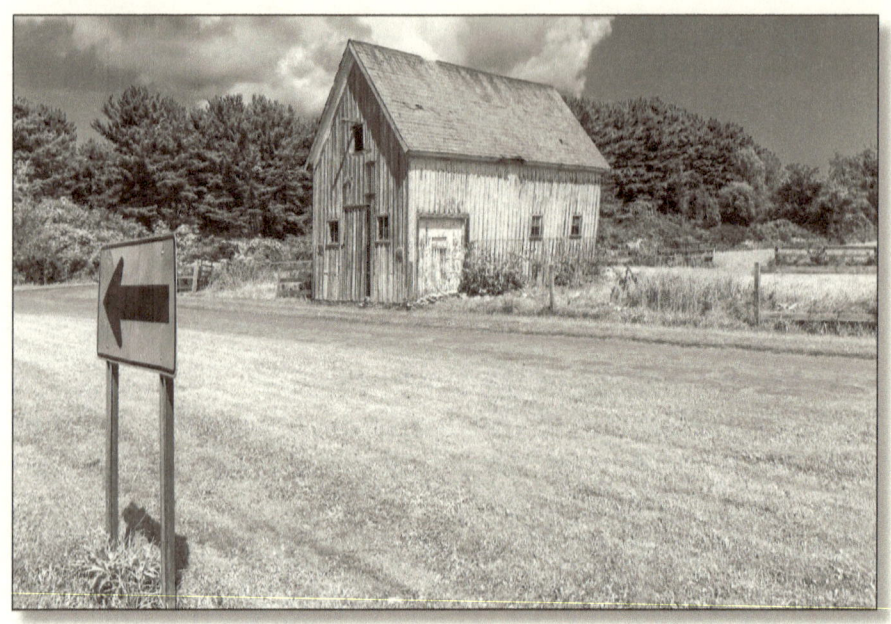

Sanford Farms, Amsterdam N.Y., Sept. 7, 2014.
Canon EOS 1DS (11.1 megapixels, full frame) 28mm, 1/320, f/11, ISO 125
© 2014, 2015 by Shawn M. Tomlinson

So, thrilled as I was, it still took many more years before all the technology caught up. I stayed working with Photoshop through it all — Digital Darkroom had hit the cutting room floor — and learned much. So much, in fact, that by the time everything did catch up and I had a DSLR and a good Mac, it showed me how wonderful post-processing could be.

I know Ansel Adams danced around the darkroom, dodging and burning, trying everything. He said something to the effect that less than half of the final photograph was taking the photograph. The majority of his work, and the thing that made his images so spectacular, was was in the darkroom.

I got really good at photo editing in Photoshop, exactly the opposite of my skill in the darkroom. I know it is easy to develop these skills and then rely upon them to "fix" less-then-perfect images on the computer.

If you're doing that all of the time, though, aren't you more of a technician than a photographer? A friend of mine, comparing his photographic work to mine admitted my skills in Photoshop, then said he believed his photos were better because he could "see" the photos, captured the photos and did little in Photoshop. He insinuated I was more of a technician than a photographer.

Which is kind of funny considering how much I had to teach him about shooting photos to get them up to a level that I could use on newspaper

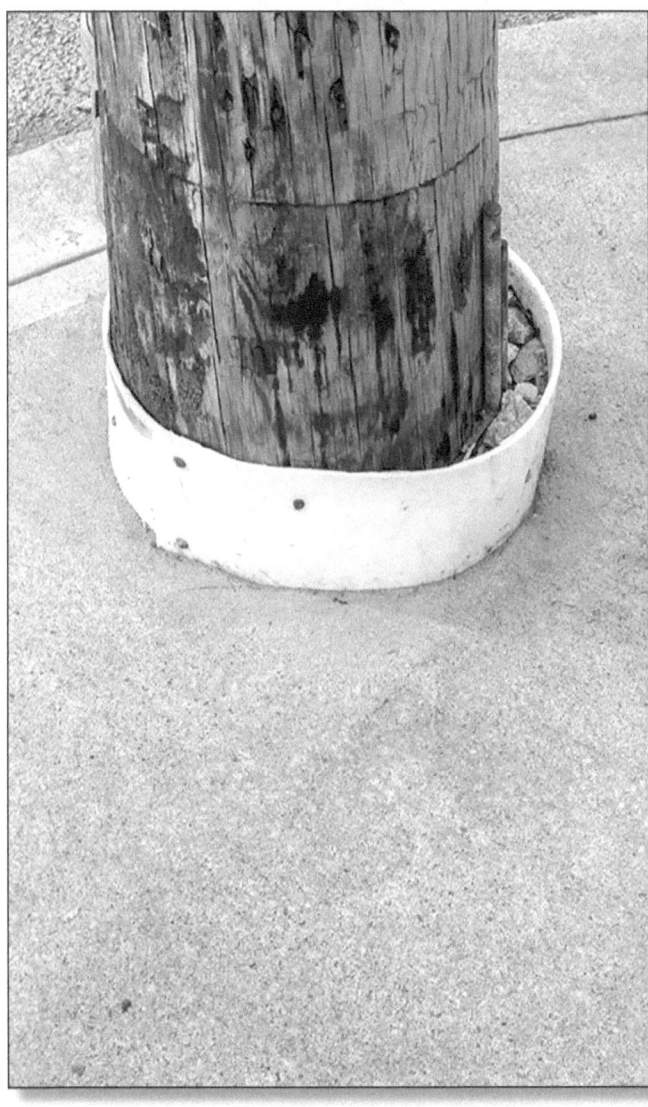

Saratoga Springs, N.Y., Oct. 28, 2014.
Nikon D7000 (16.2 megapixels), 55 mm, 1/320, f/9, ISO 250
© 2014, 2015 by Shawn M. Tomlinson

pages.

Anyway, his comments irked me, but also made me think about it.

Was he right?

Was I a mere technician who, as a photographer, shot crappy images and only made them shine in Photoshop?

I looked at many, many images shot up to that time. I concluded several things:

1) I actually am a competent, good photographer.

2) I used — perhaps — a bit too much post-production Photoshop technique.

3) I needed to cut down a

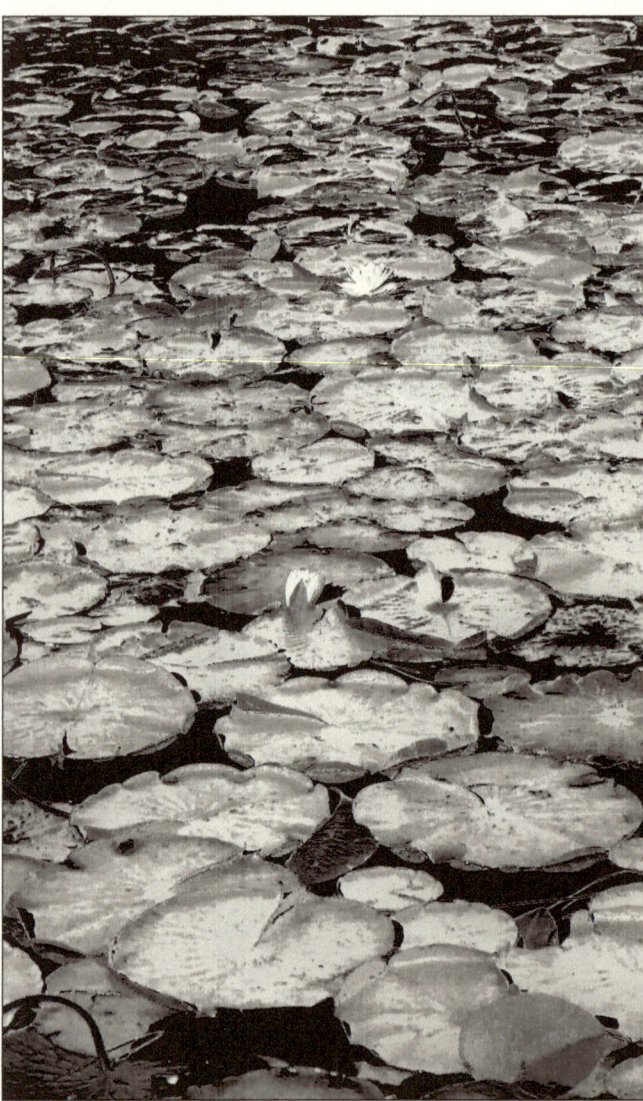

HDR Toning gone mad, Ballston Lake, N.Y., July 11, 2014.
Canon EOS 20D (8.2 megapixels), 80mm, 1/1600, f/5.6, ISO 200
© 2014, 2015 by Shawn M. Tomlinson

bit on my Photoshop "fixes."

and

4) My friend didn't do much in Photoshop because he didn't know how. I gave him some lessons and he sent me many images for "fixes" after that.

You cannot make a bad photograph great in Photoshop.

You can easily overdo post-processing. For example, I wish Adobe had not added the "HDR Toning" tool because it makes people want to use it and it makes photos look wholly unrealistic. (I thought it was "really cool" at first, then realize how crappy my HDR-toned images were. Stay away from it!)

So what is not too much?

Well, the basics.

You're shooting in RAW, ALWAYS, so you have

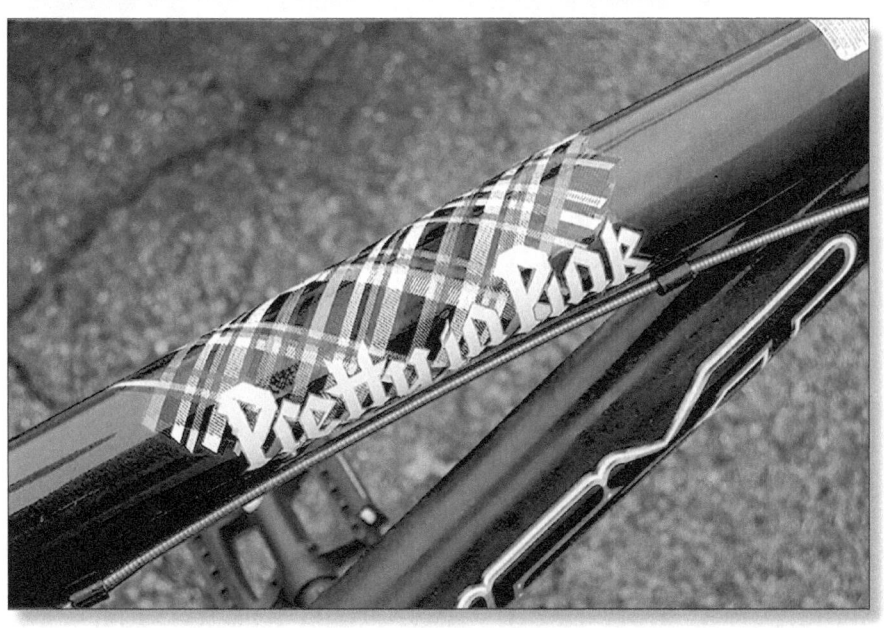

Niskayuna, N.Y., Nov. 6, 2014.
Nikon D7000 (16.2 megapixels), 55 mm, 1/400, f/6.3, ISO 400
© 2014, 2015 by Shawn M. Tomlinson

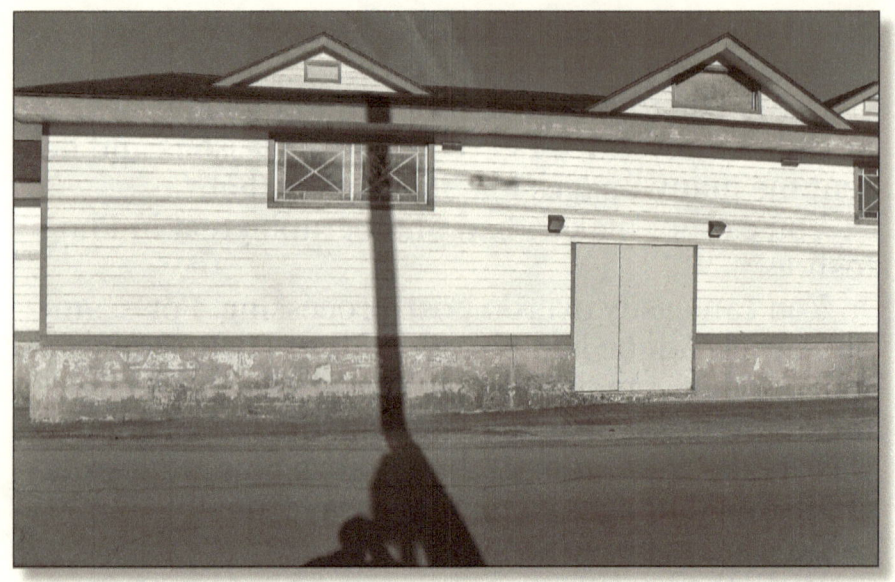

Shawn M. Tomlinson, Caroga Lake, N.Y., May 18, 2012.
Pentax *ist DS *(6.1 megapixels), 18mm, 1/350, f/11, ISO 200
© 2012, 2015 by Shawn M. Tomlinson

many possibilities in Photoshop. Don't use them all.

I do most of my "fixes" in the Camera RAW Workspace. I start by correcting lens distortion if there is any and removing chromatic aberration. I tweak the White Balance sliders only if necessary to make the image look like I saw it when I took it.

Then I do something the pros all cringe at: I hit the Auto button for Exposure.

Cringe away.

I rarely keep what Photoshop tells me should be the perfect photo adjustments, but I like to see what those adjustments are, especially because Photoshop does some good things with Contrast I probably wouldn't have thought of. It usually brings it down, which gives more detail. My instinct was to boost Contrast.

Anyway, once I've either made adjustments to Photoshop's Auto adjustments, I take the Clarity up a bit and — sometimes — boost the saturation. I then open the file in the main Photoshop pane and, occasionally, make a few adjustments from there. The main one I use is a 15 percent decrease in Highlights that I have setup as an Action. This brings out more detail in brightly lit or washed out areas.

That's it.

Size it and save it as a TIFF, I'm done.

As mentioned, this was not always what I did, but now that I use this basic set of rules, most of my photos are better and look more natural and real. I haven't touched HDR Toning in a long time.

The point is that you should rely upon your skills as a photographer much more than upon your skills as a technician. It is great to be able to make adjustments and fix minor problems in your photo editing software, but if you concentrate upon composing, exposure and shooting, you will have far fewer fixes to make.

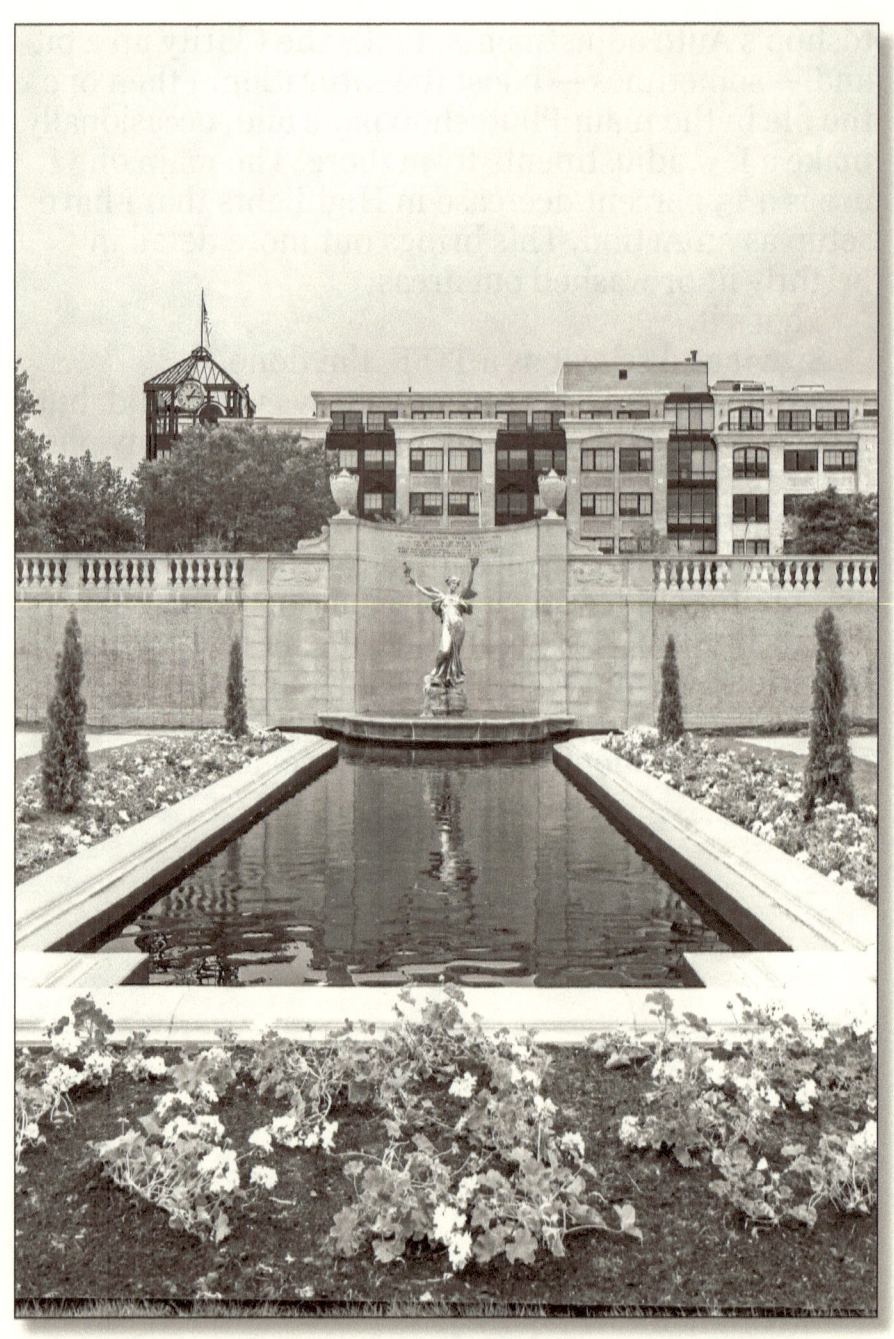

Saratoga Springs, N.Y., June 27, 2015.
Nikon D800e, 28mm, 1/1000, f/13, ISO 640, Tv, Pattern Metering
Photo © 2015 by Shawn M. Tomlinson

Rely Upon Post-Processing

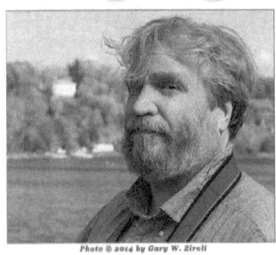

The 12
Steps of
Photography

Step
11

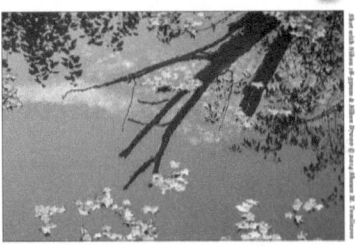

Then again, sometimes the absolute best photos you compose in the viewfinder of your DSLR don't look quite as good when they come up in the Camera RAW Workspace. They're too dark or too light or the white balance was off or something else happened.

These kinds of things will happen less the better you get as a photographer and the more familiar you become with your DSLR and its controls, but it still will happen.

And for a time, while you are experimenting, no matter how good you are, you will have some images that need something in Photoshop to make them work, too.

Experimenting is good, so keep it up, despite the extra post-processing work. It teaches you a lot.

Experimenting, too, will become less scary when you know you can make "fixes" in your photo editing software. You will feel less frustrated because you can salvage what was a good photo but had something go wrong with it.

You can't really fix blurriness, and this includes most camera shake motion blur. Photoshop does have a sharpening filter called Shake Reduction, but it only goes so far and sometimes makes photos look worse. Sometimes, if the algorithm gets carried away with itself, your images can look a bit like old 3D movies as seen without the paper-and-plastic red-and-blue glasses.

Thankfully, there's always Command-Z. That will save you many, many times.

I think it's Control-Z on a Windows-based computer, but you're a photographer, dammit, what the bloody hell are you doing using a Windows-based computer? Well?

Grow up. Get a Mac.

Ahem.

Anyway, there are times when you will need to rely upon your skills at post-processing. I do. I try to keep those times to a minimum by getting better at

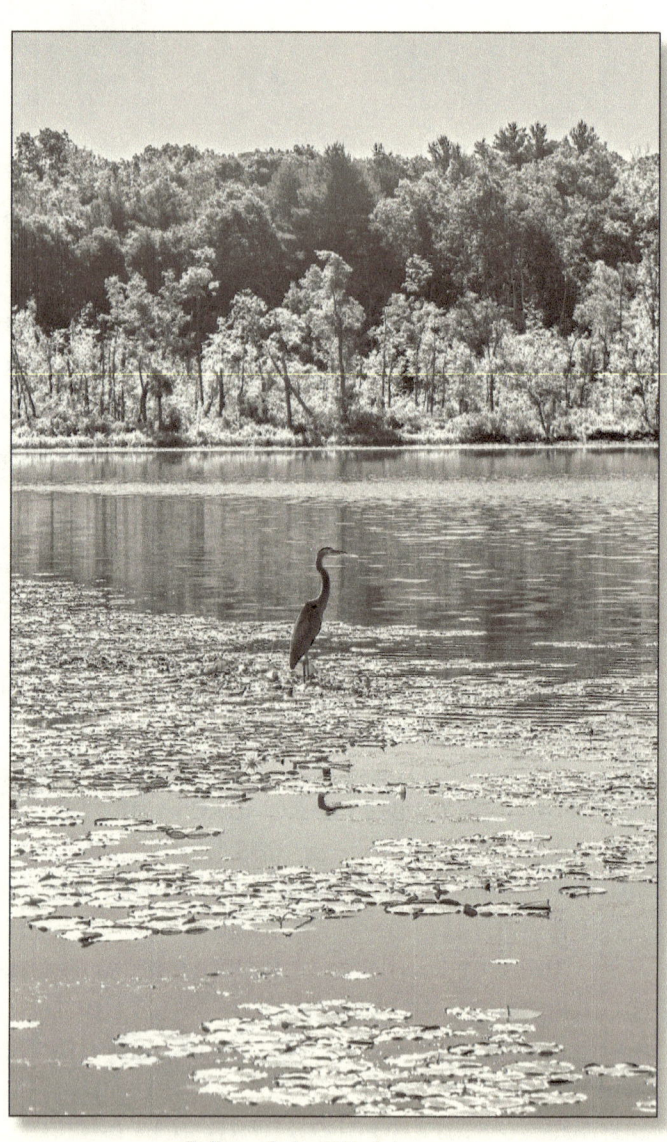

Ballston Lake, N.Y., July 11, 2014.
Canon EOS 20D (8.2 megapixels), 80mm, 1/1600, f/5.6, ISO 200
© 2014, 2015 by Shawn M. Tomlinson

taking the photos in the first place, but I do experiment and try new cameras and lenses, so not everything I "know" always works. It won't. I accept that.

The main things you may find yourself needing to fix in post-processing are exposure and white balance. These are the two most likely culprits sneaking in and disrupting your glorious Voyages of Photography.

And as you fix them, if you pay attention to the numbers of, say the White Balance Temperature, you can apply what you've learned in the DSLR while shooting.

White Balance

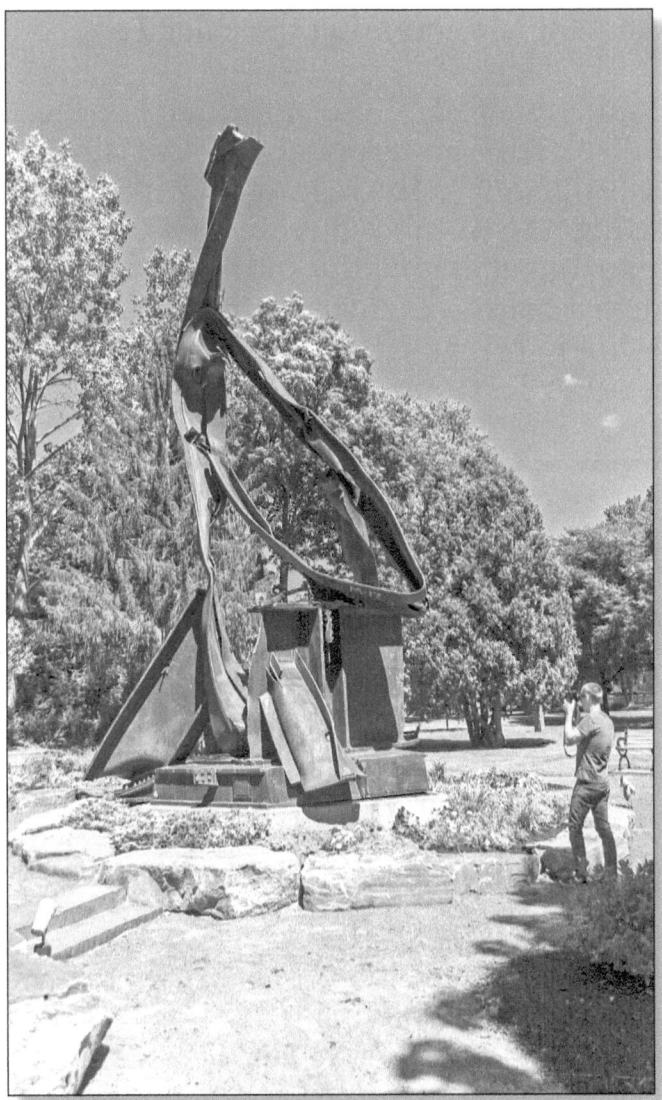

Gary Ziroli, Saratoga Springs, N.Y., Aug. 19, 2014.
Nikon D1 (2.65 megapixels), 18mm, 1/2000, f/3.5, ISO 200
© 2014, 2015 by Shawn M. Tomlinson

is one of those Zen-like things that has no right answer. For example, if I shoot on an overcast, bleak day and I hit the Cloudy White Balance preset, I get an orange-ish cast that looks like a nuclear bomb has just gone off in the distance. Not exactly what I want. Clicking Auto often makes images appear too cold by upping the blue, that is, decreasing the color Temperature.

Unless you understand and use an actual, honest-to-God-made-of-plastic-(or-cardboard) Gray Card, White Balance is difficult in the real world with your DSLR, too. Setting it to Auto in the camera works much of the time, but changing the setting — or forgetting to change it back — can cause strange color casts. In once shot in bright sunshine with the DSLR's White Balance set to Tungsten. Everything was under-

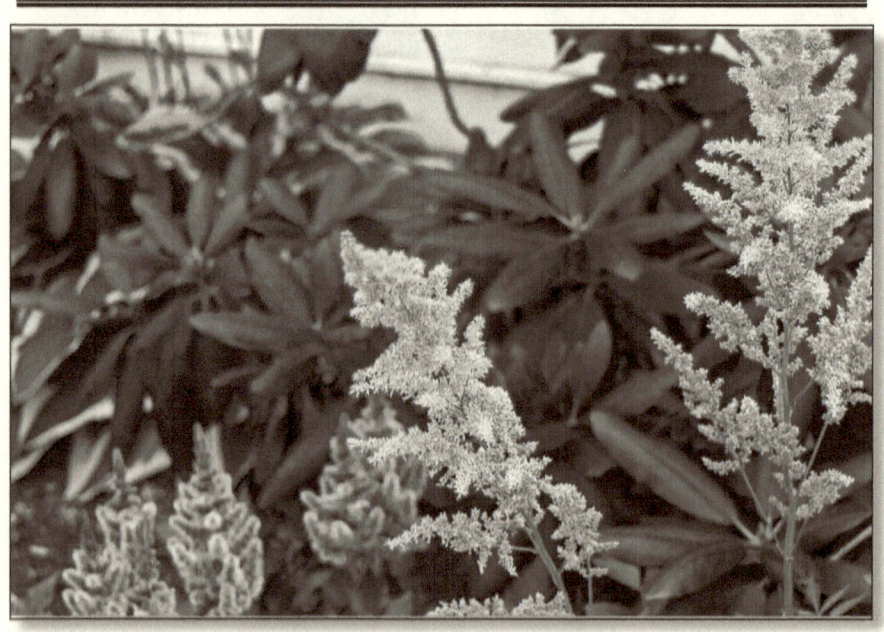

Saratoga Springs, N.Y., July 12, 2014.
Nikon D1 (2.65 megapixels), 52mm, 1/250, f/4.8, ISO 200
© 2014, 2015 by Shawn M. Tomlinson

the-sea deep blue.

You need to be careful with White Balance, yet it is a crucial ingredient of a great photo that you may have to at least tweak to make work. In Photoshop RAW terms, White Balance is essentially a combination of Color Temperature, which is Blue-to-Yellow, with Tint, which is Green-to-Magenta. It didn't make sense to me at first, but experimenting with these two sliders does get you to a natural White Balance in most cases.

Another place where relying upon post-processing is essential is spot removal.

Although I do recommend cleaning your DSLR's sensor — very, very carefully — from time to time, dust bits can get on your sensor easily, especially if you change lenses often, or even occasionally.

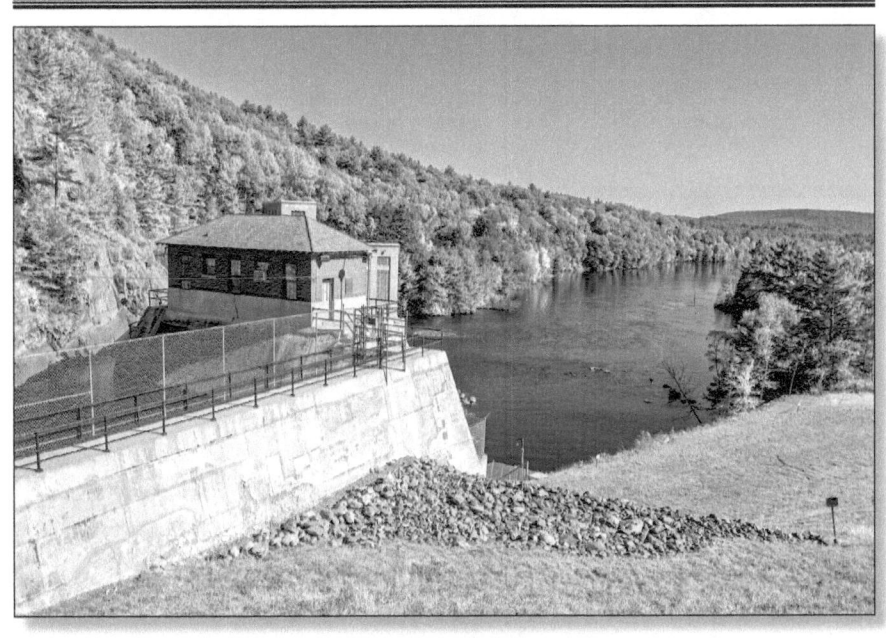

Comklingville, N.Y., Sept. 27, 2014.
Nikon D3200 (24 megapixels), 18mm, 1/1000, f/6.3, ISO 200
© 2014, 2015 by Shawn M. Tomlinson

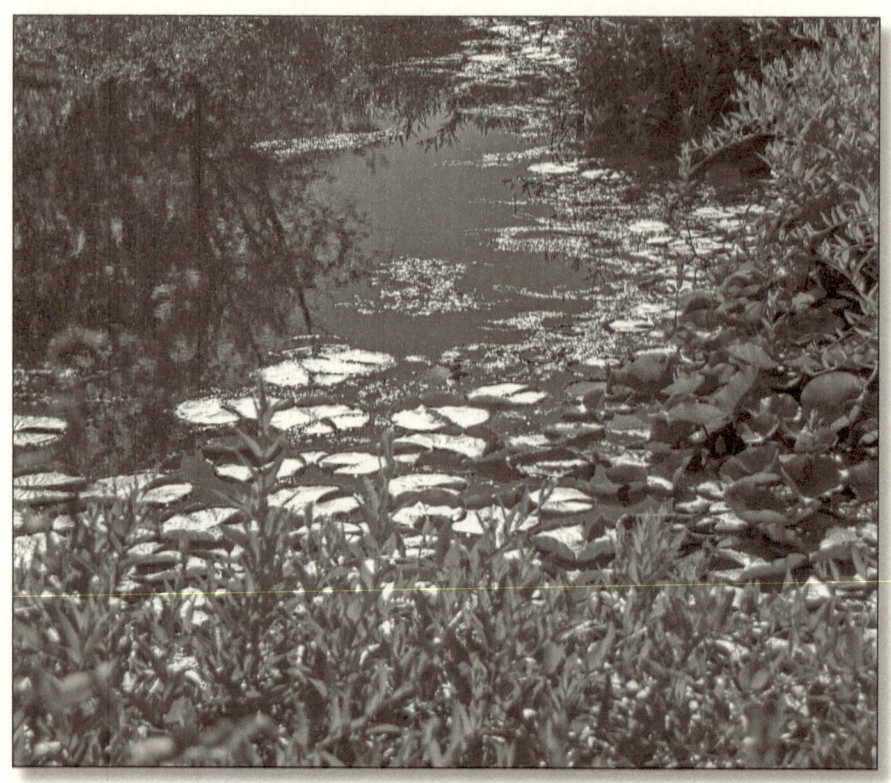

Ballston Lake, N.Y., July 11, 2014.
Canon EOS 20D (8.2 megapixels), 63mm, 1/1600, f/5, ISO 200
© 2014, 2015 by Shawn M. Tomlinson

You may not notice the spots before you head out in the field because, for example, your last batch of processed images may have been devoid of sky, water or other vast expanses of a single color or tone. Spots only typically — unless there are many and very bad — show up in sky, water, big white areas, etc.

Although most modern DSLRs have some form of sensor cleaning built in, it doesn't always work well, which leaves spots in your images.

The Clone Stamp Tool to the Rescue!

Cloning usually is the best way to get spots out of your images. It isn't difficult, even if sometimes it takes a while and can be tedious. Still, if you are going to exhibit your images, the spots should be gone.

I am constantly amazed that amateurs and pros alike often fail to remove the spots. I see "my best" type photos posted on Flickr and elsewhere by amateurs filled with spots. Worse, I see sample images by pros at photographic review sites that have spots in them.

There likely are other things that you specifically need to do in post-processing your images to get them to look the way you want them to in their final form. Certainly, rely upon your photo editing software for these things. Photoshop, Lightroom, Aperture and the free Seashore and Gimp all have essential tools for photographers. If we didn't need them, they wouldn't be there.

The point, though, is to trust to your photo editing software for the basics, but don't rely upon it to save your butt from badly composed or exposed images. It's not a miracle worker, dammit Jim, it's a photo editor.

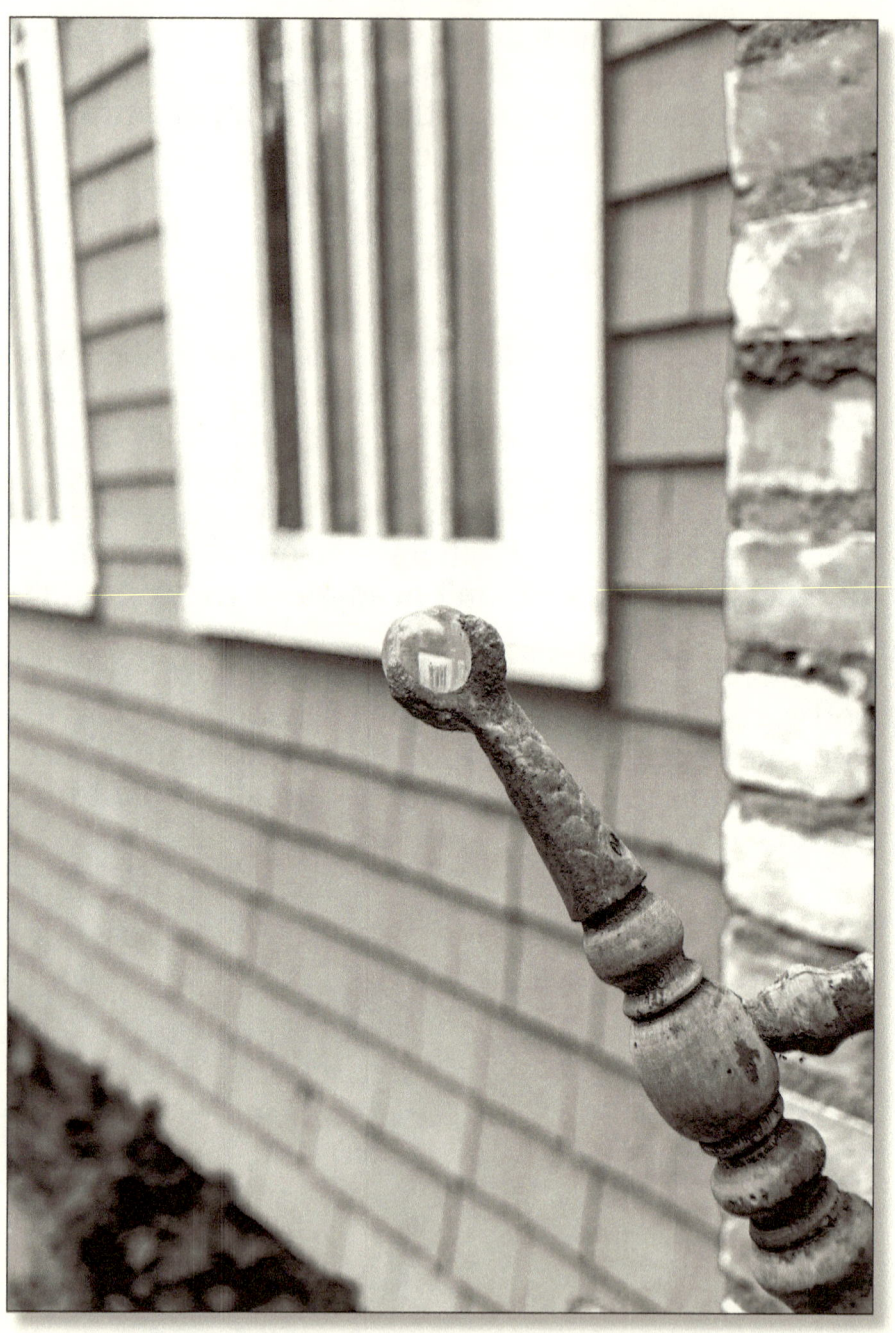

Saratoga Springs, N.Y., June 27, 2015.
Nikon D800e, 28mm, 1/800, f/4, ISO 200, Tv, Pattern Metering
Photo © 2015 by Shawn M. Tomlinson

Shoot Some More

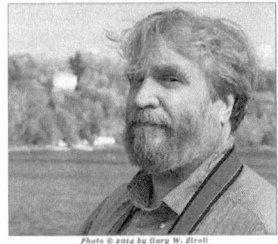

The 12
Steps of
Photography

Step
12

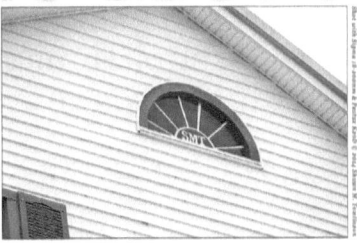

I know.

I'm being redundant.

Shoot some more.

All of the 12 Steps of Photography are important or I wouldn't have written about them and you wouldn't have read them. Each one will help you be a better photographer.

Still, the single most important step is to shoot.

All the time.

Every day.

Make a photo essay of your cat, dog or ferret. Even these simple subjects will teach you about light, shutter speed, aperture and composition.

Find objects in your home that are interesting and photograph them. Even if they are not innately interesting, look at the shadows they cast from indoor lighting or the sun streaming through the window.

Photograph your significant others. Do a portrait photo essay. Walk with him or her through a park. Have her or him play with the dog or the children or the grandchildren.

Shoot the alphabet. This is an old photo exercise, but still stretches your imagination and your photographic skills. What it means is go out or stay in and photograph individual objects that resemble the letters of the alphabet. Shoot all 26, and don't let any of them be redundant with the others. You can learn a lot from how this makes you think and see in relation to your photographic work.

Take a stroll through your neighborhood. Look at all the things you've seen a thousand times as if for the first time and with photographic possibilities in mind. Take this stroll often. Whether you live in a rural, urban or suburban area, there are endless possibilities for photographs.

Go to the next village or city over from yours. Take a friend or significant other. Take a walk along the sidewalks. Look at the stores, the

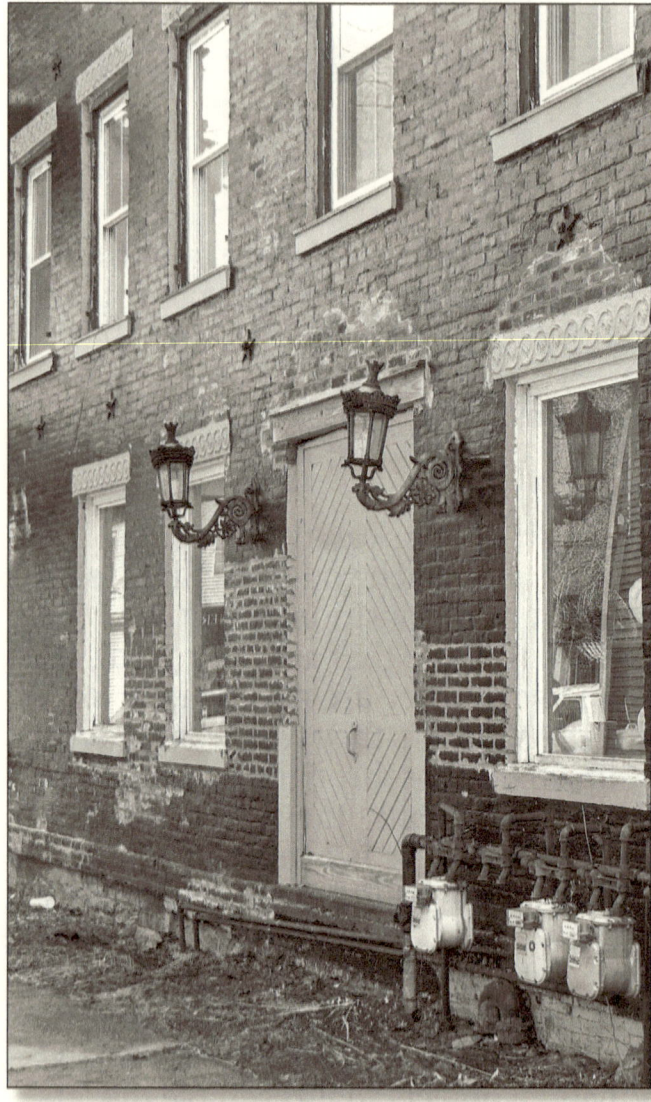

Ballston Spa, N.Y., April 12, 2014.
Pentax K20D (14.2 megapixels) 34mm, 1/250, f/6.7, ISO 280
© 2014, 2015 by Shawn M. Tomlinson

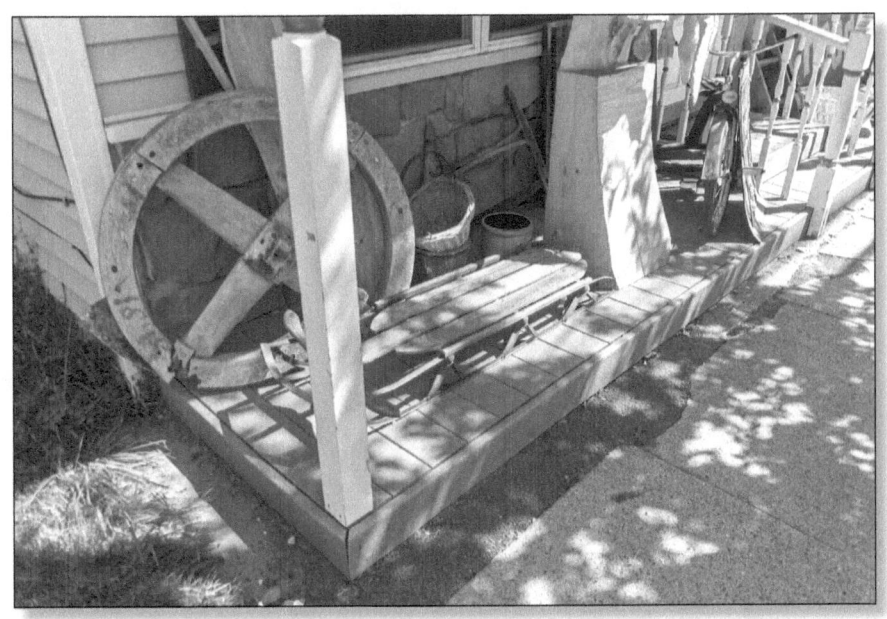

Greenwich, N.Y., Aug. 30, 2014.
Pentax K20D (14.2 megapixels) 18mm, 1/750, f/4.5, ISO 280
© 2014, 2015 by Shawn M. Tomlinson

buildings, the houses, the sidewalk, the trees poking through the sidewalks, the shadows, the graffiti, the rails, the bridges, etc.

For example, two nearby villages that my friend and photographic colleague, Gary Ziroli, and I have shot many times always yield lots of photographs. We walk the same streets and look for different ones.

These two villages are Ballston Spa and Greenwich.

Ballston Spa, founded upon the "healing" waters just like its big sister, Saratoga Springs, isn't that large. It has two ex-factories, one now in uses as a restaurant and offices, the other empty and abandoned. It has a quaint and interesting intersection of two business streets with most businesses occupying old — 1800s — buildings. Some of the artifacts of the past still exist along with the buildings. A giant Community Bulletin Board from the 1930s; painted advertisements now fading on the brick walls. The former railroad line has been turned into a walking trail. The village has antique shops, coffee and tea shops, restaurants, pizza joints, a small park dedicated to subma-

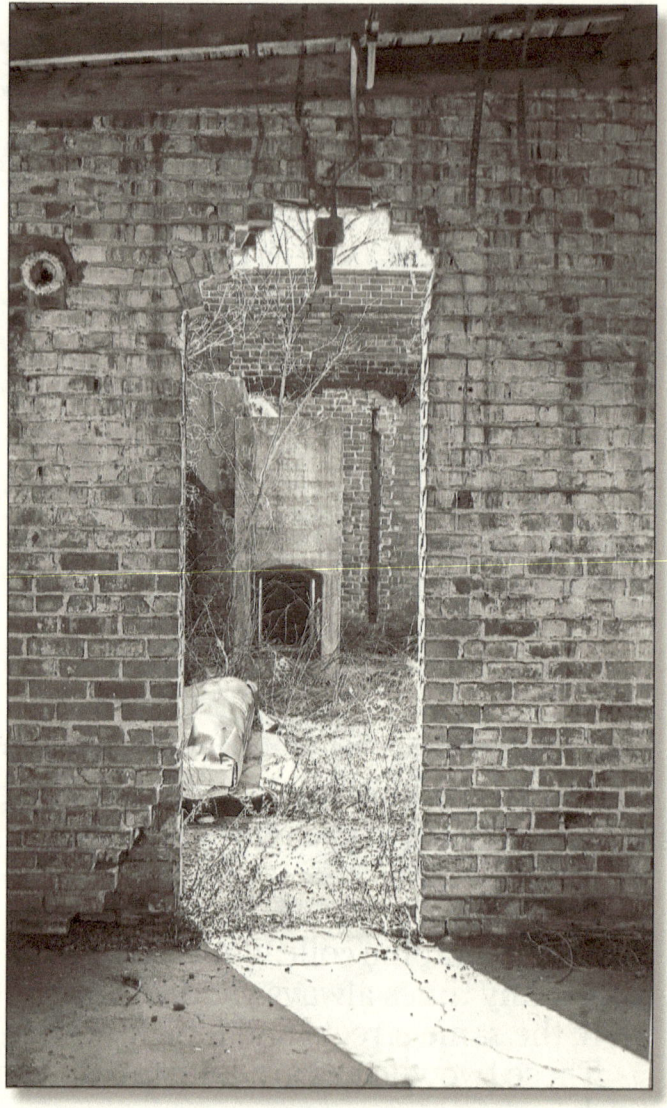

Ballston Spa, N.Y., April 12, 2014.
Canon EOS 10D (6.1 megapixels) 28mm, 1/250, f/4, ISO 200
© 2014, 2015 by Shawn M. Tomlinson

rine sailors, and many other interesting things. Atop a corner building are numerous statues of owls. In one small window at the top peak of an 1800s building, newly painted are my initials: SMT. The bowling alley just received a vivid, garish coat of paint.

One day when we were walking, a hairstylist was coming out of an 1800s red house now converted to a hair salon. She saw Gary and me, and instead of getting weird and asking what the hell we were doing — as some people do — she just started talking to us and told us there are two ghosts — a man, the builder of the house named Samuel; and an unknown woman — hanging around in certain rooms of the building. She invited us to come back and try to photograph them and the inside of the building if we liked.

Greenwich, to the east of Saratoga Springs, is like a lone oasis in the middle of a very rural farming area. It once was a thriving, all-on-its-own village, but now has turned many storefronts over to antique shops. The in-village grocery stores are gone, but a

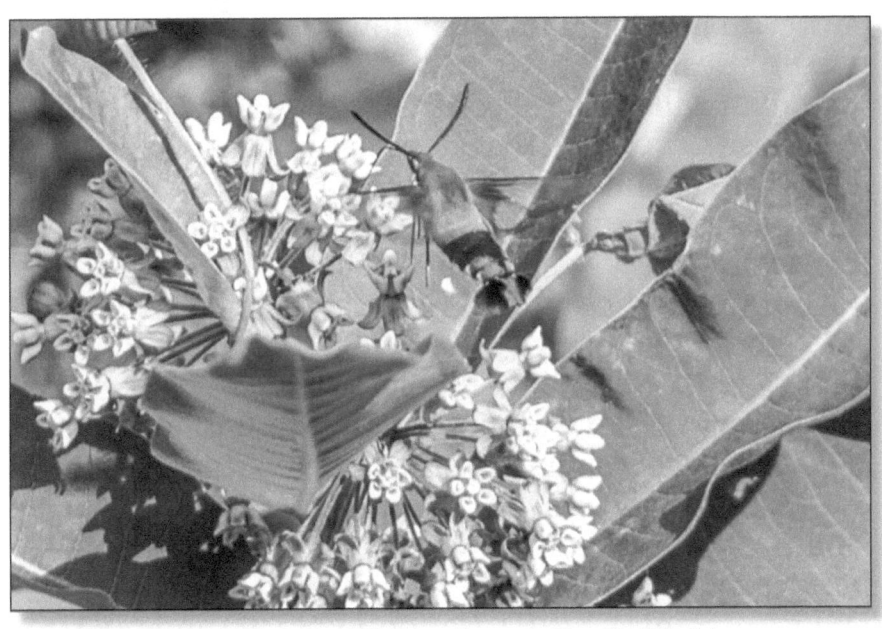

Hummingbird Moth, Indian Kill Nature Preserve, Glenville, N.Y., July 21, 2014.
Nikon D1 (2.65 megapixels), 80mm, 1/350, f/5.6, ISO 200
© 2014, 2015 by Shawn M. Tomlinson

Hannaford Supermarket and a very small Kmart exist at the western entrance. In Greenwich, we've found several very interesting locations. There is, of course, the main street, which never fails to intrigue us, especially the big, long empty house that we would both love to get inside to shoot. Apart from the main street, the side streets have everything from rich, big houses, to poor ex-factory housing. At the end of the main street at the east are two old railroad trestles, one with a short tunnel underneath that leads to an old factory and a separate enclave of houses. Around the curve and down a dead end street, a small park abuts the Batten Kill River and the dam built there, as well as the village waterworks. The Steep cliff on the other side of the of the river affords a view of the river and the dam.

The village is filled with old churches and their steeples, a dark forbidding cemetery, a three-sided park with great and unusual flowers, and many other possibilities.

Indian Kill Nature Preserve within a few miles of my house never fails to yield great images, at least a few, even in winter. It consists of a series of hiking trails, a stream in a deep valley and the opportunity to stretch your legs climbing back out of the valley. At the bottom of the railroad tie twisted, craggy stairs, a steel-and-wood bridge extends over a waterfall. It's a man-made water fall that looks like it once was part of a factory or some other structure, but there are no signs and research has left the mystery intact.

No matter the season, Indian Kill has endless possibilities. I rarely come out with fewer than a couple hundred photographs. I've shot it with nearly all my DSLRs — Pentax K20D, Canon EOS 10D and 20D, Nikon D1, D70 and D7000 — had gotten great if different results with all of them. It is the place I first took the D1 away from the house when I had no charger and had to shoot with the camera plugged into an AC/DC converter plugged into the car's outlet. It limited motion, but it was the first set of images from the camera that proved to me that, as old as it was, it still was quite good. Months later, with a working battery, I took the D1 back to Indian Kill and ventured into the valley. My 300-plus images from that day include some of a critter I never had heard of or seen before, a hummingbird moth.

My point with all these anecdotal description lists is to show you just a fraction of the types of possibilities you can find nearby. You may not live near these same places, but you live some place, and I guarantee you, you can find interesting photographic subjects there.

You just need to get out and look.

And shoot some more.

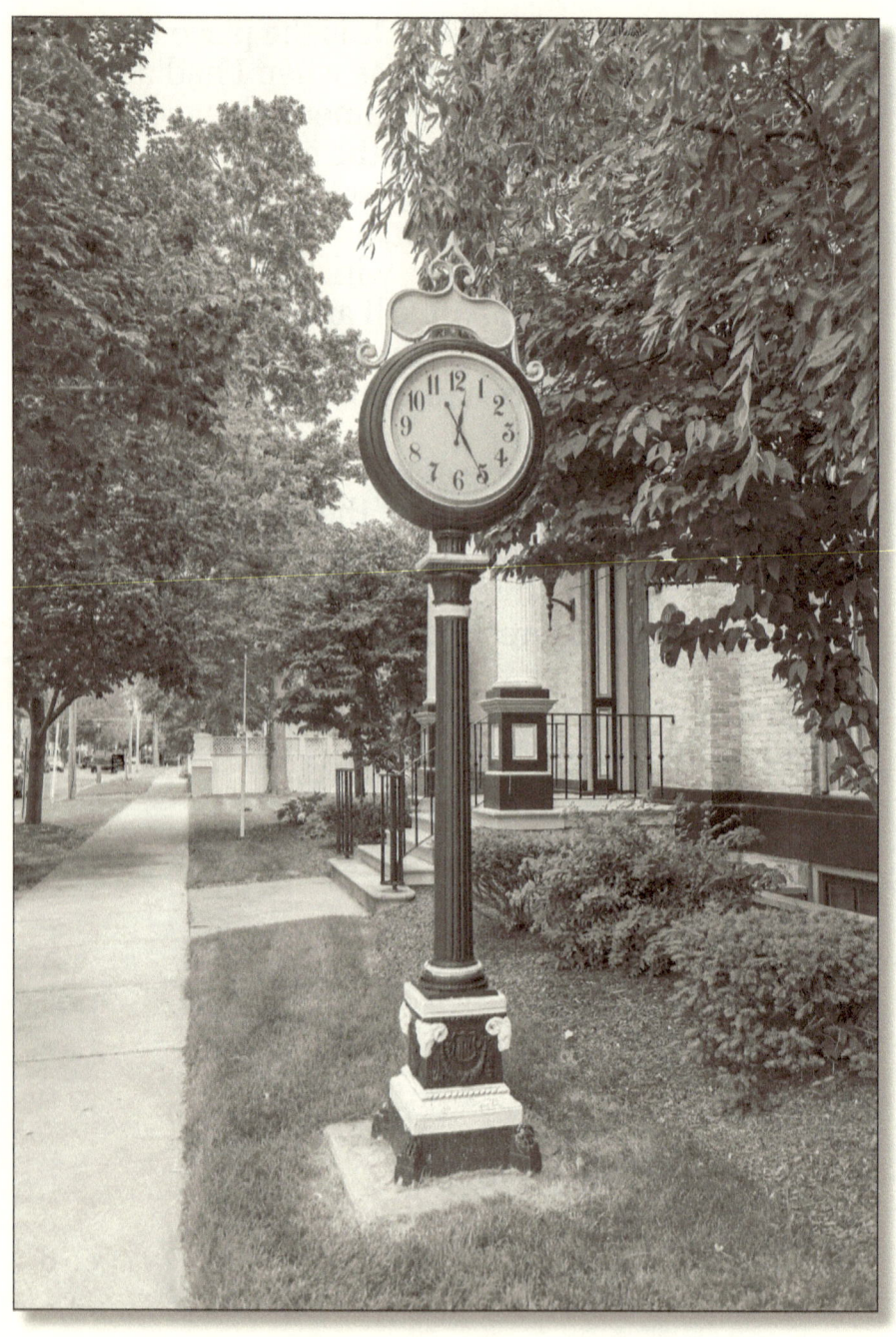

Saratoga Springs, N.Y., June 27, 2015.
Nikon D800e, 28mm, 1/1000, f/5.6, ISO 640, Tv, Pattern Metering
Photo © 2015 by Shawn M. Tomlinson

Last Words

There's not a lot more to say, but I'm sure that won't stop me from writing much more about photography.

These 12 Steps to Photography are not hard and perfect rules, but you probably guessed that already. They simply are guidelines and ideas to help you to help yourself to become a better photographer.

And we all want to become better photographers.

I get email tips from PictureCorrect.com nearly every day. I usually read them, but at this point they often are redundant... for me. For someone just starting his or her photographic voyage, they probably are new and eye-opening, as I'm sure some of what I've written here will be.

Teaching photography is somewhat like teaching writing. I can give you the basics as well as what I've learned over the years, but you must develop your own style and idiom.

There is no way to teach you how to take breathtaking photographs. That you must find on your own.

However, the advice and tools provided here can help you along the way to that breathtaking photo goal because using them will give you control over and confidence in your photographic talent and skills.

That's my goal.

Use what works for you, toss what doesn't.

That's the way to develop yourself as a photographer.

Oh, yeah, and remember:

Shoot!

Have at it.

— Shawn M. Tomlinson

Shawn M. Tomlinson's Guide to Photography Series

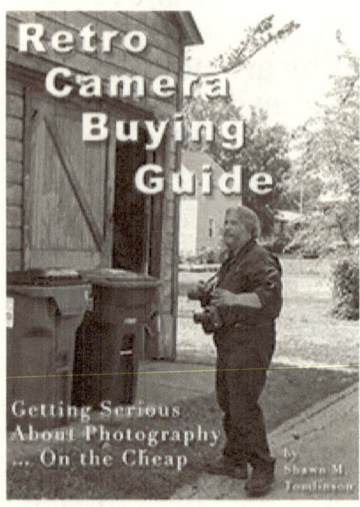

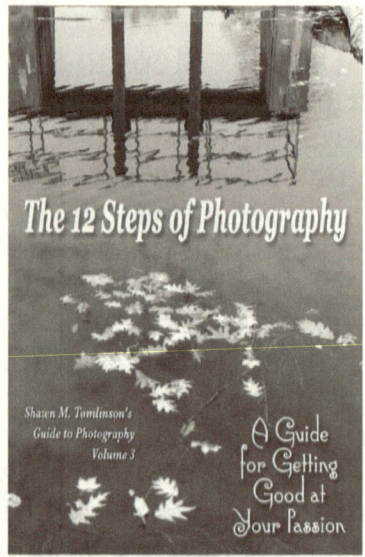

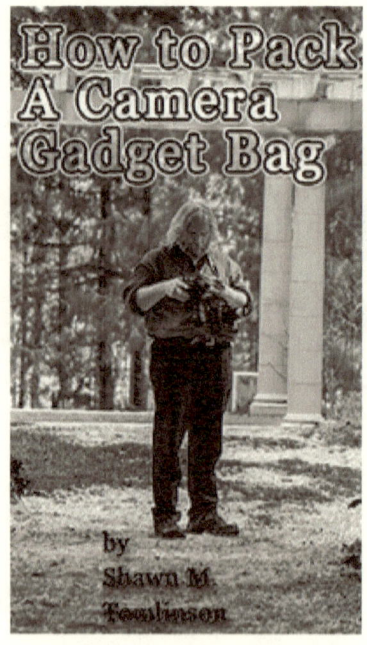

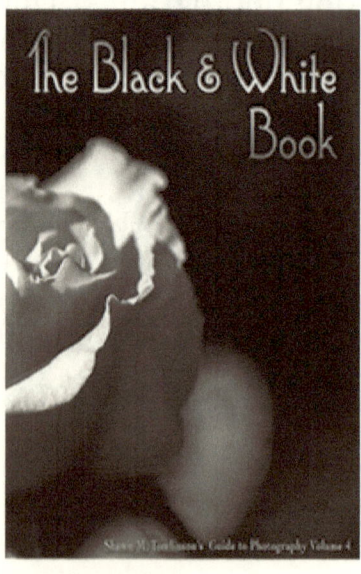

Shawn M. Tomlinson's Guide to Photography Series

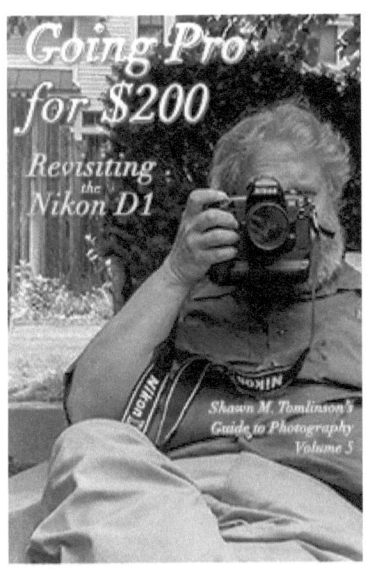

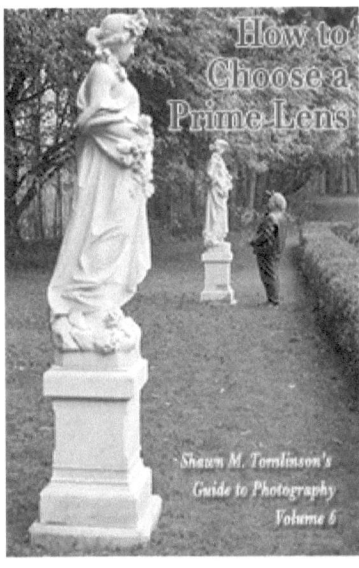

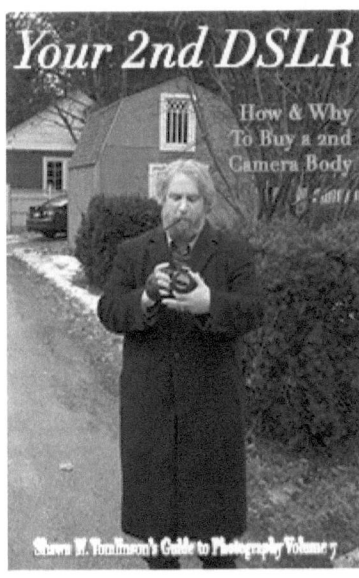

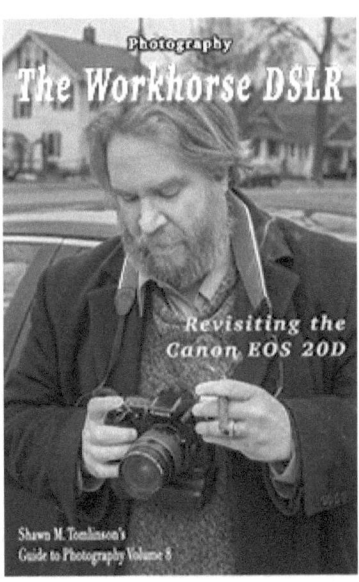

Shawn M. Tomlinson's Guide to Photography Series

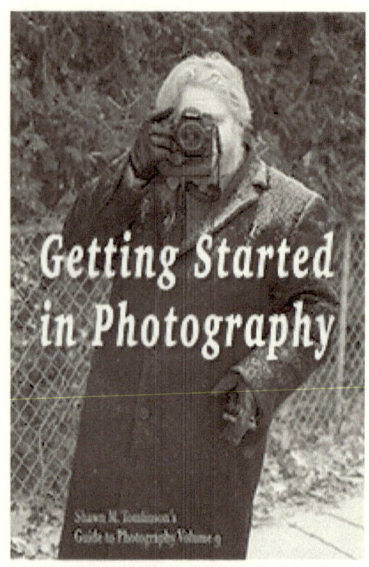

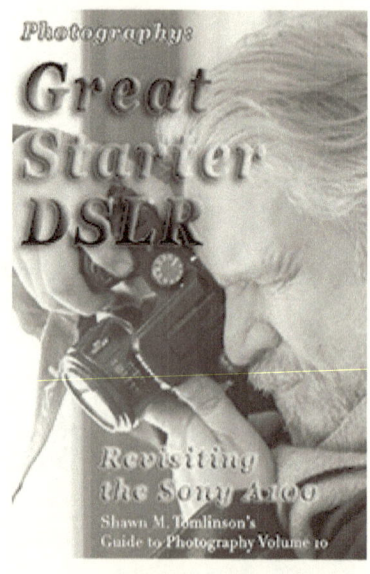

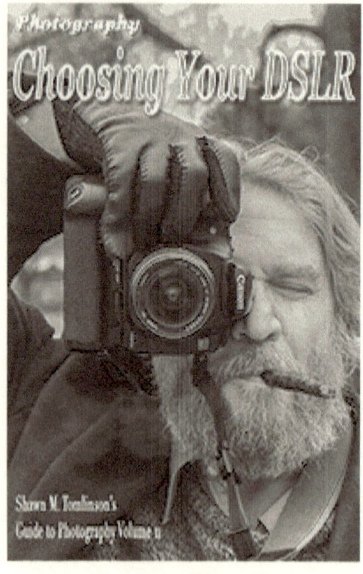

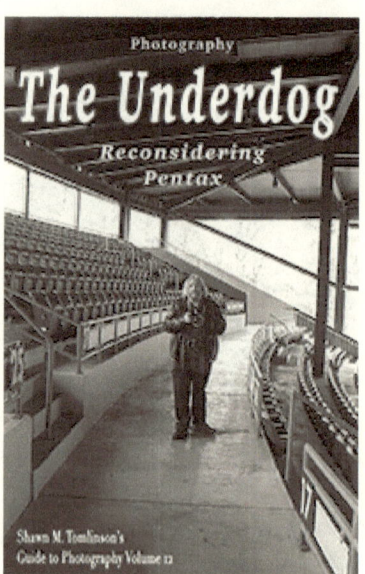

The Photo Curmudgeon

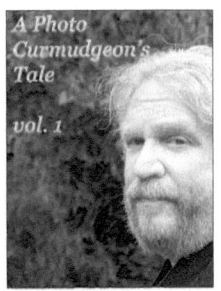

A Photo Curmudgeon's Tale Volume 1

The first 25 Photo Curmudgeon columns collection covering everything photographic also includes several columns that preceded the Curmudgeon. Includes many photographs to illustrate points in the columns.

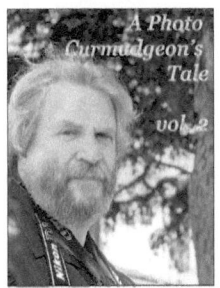

A Photo Curmudgeon's Tale Volume 2

The second 25 Photo Curmudgeon columns collection covering everything photographic considers lenses, cameras, photo editing techniques, locations and more.

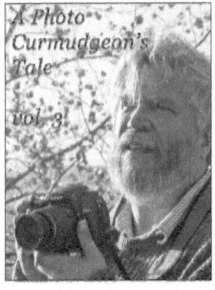

A Photo Curmudgeon's Tale Volume 3

Photo Curmudgeon columns 051-075 are collected in this third volume covering everything photographic including lenses, cameras, photo editing techniques, locations and more.

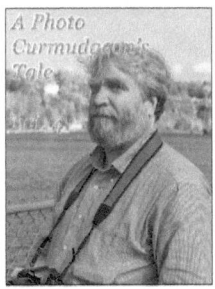

A Photo Curmudgeon's Tale Volume 4

Photo Curmudgeon columns 076-100 complete the fourth volume of the collection with insights about Nikon, Canon, Pentax DSLRs, prime lenses, seeking locations and technique among other topics.

www.ingramcontent.com/pod-product-compliance
Lightning Source LLC
Chambersburg PA
CBHW022059170526
45157CB00004B/1409